she

THE GRACE PARABLES

Cover photography by Hollie Marie Photography

For more writings by Jess, visit her blog.

jess-hays.com

Contact Jess at vagabondminister@gmail.com

For Mom

The first "She" who taught me the significance and power of being both fragile and fierce. You are a beautiful smudge of grace on the canvas of my life.

CONTENTS

Introduction

What is Grace?

Grace.

This word has become wildly overused in the modern church. It's become an expression of the warm tingly feelings we undeservingly get from God. Many make "grace" synonymous with the word "blessing" others with the word "forgiveness" but grace is something bigger than that. We've reduced it to a platitude, a cliché Christian catchphrase, an acronym to hang on our church walls, and in doing so we have reduced it to a piece of our religion rather than the very essence of our life.

I can only write these things because I am so very guilty of doing them myself. I have recently become convinced that Satan, knowing he cannot silence truth, does the next best thing—he spams us with alternative truths. If he cannot suppress the bigness of God's grace then he offers us many alternative definitions of it. Grace then becomes so common place in our language we rarely are aware of its power. So, before you get into the grace parables that follow, I want to offer a bigger and clearer view of God's amazing grace as I have experienced it.

I used to view grace as a concept, an action, something that God did or something that God gave. I've asked others what they think grace is and some would say, "we are saved by grace," so then grace is simply about Jesus's death on the cross and my actions are up to me. Oh, my friends, let me tell you it is so much more.

I have come to understand that grace is God's expression of His identity. Grace is God's pouring out of who He is on to us. Grace is not only God's action but also God's essence. Grace then is not what God DOES but rather WHO God IS. Andrew Farley says, "To say you can have too much grace is to say you can have too much godliness. They are one in the same." You cannot separate God and grace. They are one; grace is simply who God is. To know grace is to experience God.

Grace is radical. It's scandalous. May we never buy into the lie that grace is a tame entity. For it is both ruin and restoration. It will destroy all you have built and create that which you are unable to. It is a hurricane and we must resign to capsize beneath its waves.

For the self-righteous it is destruction, leaving the wreckage of our greatest efforts in its wake as it tears through our poorly built castles. We clamor for credit and it steals all the glory. For the self-loathing it is creation, birthing new identity from the ruin of our own poor choices that have led us to wander in homelessness along the beach. We ache for significance and it gives us its glory.

The storybook of my life is covered in the ink stained finger prints of grace. My white pages that I worked so hard to keep clean have been ruined by the coffee stains of God's identity. Each and every story I foolishly lay claim to has been painted over with the brush strokes of His artistic essence. I am but a victim of His glory, ravished by His love before I even knew such beauty existed.

The stories in this book are pictures of this grace. Each one is a previously white page that grace has splashed itself across. Each of these stories is designed to explore a different expression of grace, a different piece of God's identity. What follows are a collection of allegories, and though they are fictional stories they are very much based on my real and formidable struggles. They are, what I like to call, rest stops along the road of my life.

I first began writing these pieces as part of my second stint in therapy. They were a way for me to resolve the otherwise tangled and messy ball of emotions of my reality. I found that creating stories based in the reality of my own personal darkness brought a measure of order to the chaos of real life. I never intended to share them with anyone much less publish them for the world to thumb through, but as I began to share them with trusted friends and family a tickle began deep within my being. This small glimmering thought flickered annoyingly demanding my attention until finally I looked at it, and the more I looked at it the more I saw a need to share these stories.

Struggle and heartache are both fierce realities in my life and I refuse to ignore these entities. You will see the characters between these pages hurt and fight and fail because I have experienced all of those things. My greatest desire is that you will see that the story doesn't end there. I long to express the unimaginable hope that arises to steal away despair's story. Just as I refuse to be silent on the reality of brokenness, I also cannot help but shout of the liberating reality that is hope and rescue.

Each time you crack the spine of this book you are drawing back the curtain to look into the most intimate and vulnerable parts of my humanity, and I am certain that you will see the stains that grace has left upon them. Between these pages you will read of a Deity with dirty hands and tattooed arms and of a girl who can't help but be in awe of Him.

I hope that you will find pieces of your own story glued into the mosaic of my own. I wish for you to be encouraged both by the truth that you are not the only one who experiences brokenness and by the bigger truth that God is madly in love with all that you are.

THE TATTOOED MAN

A parable of captivity and rescue

"So often times it happens that we live our lives in chains
and we never even know we have the key"

-The Eagles

"I do not at all understand the mystery of grace—only that it
meets us where we are but does not leave us where it found
us."

-Anne Lamott

She sat in the familiar darkness; her body curled up as small as she could make it. She trembled as the cold tingling of the harsh stone floor forced itself against her exposed flesh. The musty smell of oppression and unbathed skin filled the air and she longed for freedom from this place. She had been here for so long. Here in this dark unkempt cell. She had resigned from cries for help for some time now deciding that it was pointless to wish for anything other than confinement.

This was her home now, this prison. The most unbearable part of her incarceration was not the hard floor or the wretched smell. It wasn't the constant darkness. The worst part of it all was how alone she was. Silence shook her very soul and she longed for someone, anyone, to just be with her. Soon... she stopped longing for anything. She became content in captivity.

One day, something changed. She looked up from her hunched position in the corner to see something she had not seen in a long time. So long, in fact, that she had all but forgotten what it was. There, far at the end of her prison hallway, glimmering slightly in the distance, was a light. She squinted her eyes as she strained to see where it was coming from. Even stranger still, it seemed that the more she looked at it the closer it got.

Soon it shone from the entryway, rays of light licking the hard concrete of her cell and she hid her eyes as its brilliance blinded her. Her hands cupped tightly over her eyes, she could see slightly through her fingers that the light was directly in front of her now. She felt the warmth of it kiss her skin.

Suddenly two strong hands grabbed hers and gently pulled them away from her eyes. For a moment she was blinded, but as her eyes adjusted slowly, the figure of a man faded into view. He was a muscular man with thick arms that were covered in beautifully artistic tattoos. A five o'clock shadow covered his face and his short brown hair was wild and ungroomed. He wore tattered jeans and a dirt stained white tank top. His eyes were soft and kind and his mouth stretched into a smile that she gawked at. Those eyes... they looked past her, straight into the depths of her spirit, and without him even saying a word she knew that he loved her.

Tears made streaks down her soot covered cheeks. He reached up and softly wiped them away with calloused hands, and she caught a glimpse of the scars that marked his wrists. "Don't cry, love," he whispered to her softly, his eyes filled with compassion. She said nothing. She just buried her face in his shoulder and wept. His burly arms wrapped her up tightly as her heaving sobs echoed off the walls of her cell.

When her tears finally stopped he looked down at her cradled in his arms and said, "It's time for you to be free." At first, panic knotted in the pit of her stomach, but then he took her hand in his. "Come on, follow me." His voice untangled the now web of emotions wrapped around her stomach.

Slowly, she got to her feet, grasping tightly to his rough hand intertwined in hers. Carefully he led her out of her cell, down the dark and narrow hallway, out the heavy doors of the prison, and into a beautiful field covered in tall grass and fragrant flowers. The wind caressed her skin and the sun overwhelmed her with warmth. The sweet smell of flowers and freedom assaulted her nostrils.

She let go of his hand and ran rantipole through the field until finally she collapsed peacefully on the soft grass. He laid down beside her and they stared up at the stunningly blue sky dotted with bright white clouds.

She laid her head on his chest and listened to the rhythmic thumping of his heart looking adoringly up at him. "You are free now," he said, "You never have to go back to that place." She nodded silently and snuggled into his chest. He squeezed her tightly, kissed her forehead, and whispered, "You will never be alone again. I promise." A sigh of security left her lungs and she dared to believe him.

THE WOMAN OF DARKNESS

A parable of hopelessness

"Happiness can be found even in the darkest of times if one
only remembers to turn on the light."

-Albus Dumbledore

"The moment comes when our eyes are opened, and we see
and realize that grace is infinite. Grace, my friends, demands
nothing from us but that we shall await it with confidence
and acknowledge it in gratitude."

-Isak Dineseen

That darkness, oh that darkness. How it gnawed at her soul. Some would say that she lived her life in the shadows, but even shadows leave room for light. No, that luxury had long been forfeited. There were no shadows, there were no glimmers, only darkness.

For some time, when the darkness first came, she lived in terror of it. She fought with all her might to run from it, to escape the shadows as they closed in on her, but soon shadows became darkness and she resigned to it. Now she had lived in darkness for so long that she rarely dreamed of the light. Hope for another life had been forgotten. In fact, if she were honest, she would say that she had become comfortable in the darkness.

There she lived the life she was accustomed to, a whirlwind of darkness and chaos, dimming the lives she bumped into along the way. She sometimes wished for it not to be so. But it was. And there was no use crying over it.

One day, while she was distracted by her darkness, something different happened. As she was sadly sulking feeling especially sorry for herself, her sorrow was sabotaged by a sudden explosion of light. She fell immediately to her knees as the burning brightness blinded her. Nowhere that she turned could she find escape from it; the light had overwhelmed her world.

She shut her eyes tightly grasping at a small comfort from the familiarity of the darkness. She squeezed them closed as hard as she could but small rays of light sneaked their way through the smallest of crevasses. She tore off a piece of her shirt, fashioning it into a blindfold. Darkness once again relieved her.

Why is this happening? What is this? What did I do to deser-

Her self-pitying thoughts were interrupted by two warm hands grabbing her shoulders. She flinched. It had been so long since she had felt the warmth of a gentle touch; cold governs the darkness. It made her feel awkward and uncomfortable. She jerked away in fear.

"Hey, it's ok, I'm not here to hurt you." A scruffy, masculine voice kindly reassured her.

"Wha… What do you want?" she managed to stutter out, trembling.

"I want to help you," the man answered, "I want to teach you how to live in the light."

She was confused by the thought of being helped. She had been alone in the darkness for so long. How incomprehensible it was to think of being aided. Why would she want help anyway? She was, after all, a strong independent woman.

"I'm blinded by this light. I can't even see you! How am I supposed to know if you're telling the truth?"

"I guess you'll just have to trust me." She could hear the smile in his voice as he answered her doubting inquiry.

She thought for a moment as she weighed her options. She was unable to see, to move, to do much of anything but sit there in her blindness. She would surely end up dead of she stayed there. But who was this person and why did he want to help her? What if it was a trick? She would surely end up dead if she trusted him. And if she dared to trust again and she was betrayed? Well, then she would welcome death. But what if? What if he was telling the truth? Could she dare again to hope?

So, with what little strength she had left, she did indeed dare to hope for it seemed that in her weakness she had no choice but to rely on another's strength.

"Ok. I guess, um, I guess I'll let you help me." she was hesitant.

"I will not let you down," he was resolute.

"Yeah... I've heard that before," she shot back cynically.

He chuckled a little, "Yes, I know."

She quickly tried to change the subject, ignoring how well he seemed to know her.

"So how do we do this? Are there like steps or a checklist or something? Maybe some kind of 'living in the light' crash course I can take?"

He laughed loudly. His laugh was deep and bellowing, much like the roar of a lion, but it did not evoke fear in the same way.

"Oh no, love, there is no list. There are no steps to complete or workbooks to fill out. The work has been done. You must do only one thing now." His tone was calm but exuded authority.

"What do I have to do?" she questioned with worry in her voice.

He took her hand in his and answered softly, "Rest. Trust me to do the work and free you. Let me take off your blindfold."

A tickle of fear shot across her stomach. Blood rushed to her legs and her muscles tightened ready to run. But that voice… there was something about that voice. Something that she couldn't explain. Something that made her want to believe him.

"Maybe…" she said tentatively, "…but not yet."

"I can wait," he said, his voice saturated in understanding.

And he did.

He waited as she fought him.
He waited as she doubted him.
He waited for her because to him she would always be worth the wait.

Even so, she did not dare forsake the comfort of darkness for the uncertainty of the light.

THE MAN OF LIGHT

A parable of patience

"It is the nature of grace to fill the places which have been empty."

-Goeth

"Grace means that your spirituality is upheld by God's stubborn enjoyment of you."

-Preston Sprinkle

The light. Oh how it radiated with life, with warmth, with power. That place had been his home since before time began. It was a place of hope, abundant in love, and overflowing with authenticity. He had left that world long ago. He left. He left that place of comfort and security and power. He left it. For what, you ask? He left his life of light to walk in the darkness amongst the dead.

Confusing, I know, for who would willingly choose such a life? Yet, he did. Some say he did it because he pitied them, the dead, and the death that they were tricked into. Others say he did it for praise; so that men would sing of his sacrifice for ages to come; so that his glory could be gawked at. So which was it?

If you asked him he would tell you it was for love, a great and powerful love with which he loved them. A love that could not sit enjoying the light while darkness held them captive. So he went into the darkness carrying life with him. He went to set them free.

And where he tread, darkness fled, for it had claim not even to the dirt that dusted his shoes. And light exploded around him.

Finally, he found her, the woman he loved the most. He had searched for her for some time now. There she was; damaged, depressed, and living in the darkness that she had become accustomed to. She believed that she had mastered it, but as is often true for those of her world, that which she retreated to for control, in fact, controlled her.

His heart broke for her and he took off full speed towards her, the closer he got the faster he ran, until finally he came crashing into her. His light overwhelmed her darkness.

He watched as she fell to her knees, frantically searching for the familiarity of darkness. She made a covering for her eyes holding desperately to the darkness that had become comfortable. The tears of fear streaming down her cheeks were too much for him to bear. He reached out to touch her.

She flinched at his foreign touch questioning his intentions.

"I want to help you," he pleaded genuinely, "Let me show you how to live in the light."

She doubted him and he was not surprised. The dead always doubted him. For when light shines into darkness, darkness cannot comprehend it. He was as patient as he was kind and was not dissuaded by her doubt.

You'll just have to trust me," he said with a smile.

He looked at her adoringly as she tried to decide whether or not to trust him. He found her quite extraordinary and was excited for her freedom. He was adamantly decided that he would fight for her liberty no matter what her answer was.

"I guess I will let you help me," she said still unsure.

He furrowed his brow resolutely, "I will not let you down. I promise."

Again she doubted him, but he did not balk. He knew of her pain.

Immediately she did what people always do when offered a free gift. She began searching for a way to earn it. She suggested lists and plans and booklets with rules to follow. She thought of steps and classes that she could take, what she could do to achieve this life of light, and she was unaware of how useless such things were. At this he did not get angry. He did not scold or criticize her silliness. He did what he always does, he loved her. He loved her and from that love he offered her a solution.

"Oh no, love, there is no list. There are no steps to complete or workbooks to fill out. The work has been done. You must do only one thing now." She leaned in with anticipation as he spoke.

"What do I have to do?" she questioned him and he could hear the trepidation in her voice.

He took her hand in his and answered softly, "Rest. Trust me to do the work and free you. Let me take off your blindfold."

The color faded from her face and her forehead creased with lines of anxiety. He watched with sadness as fear once again became her master. A third time she doubted him.

"Maybe..." she said cautiously, "...but not yet."

"I can wait." he said, his voice saturated in understanding.

And he did.

He waited. Not only did he wait, but for the months that followed he spent every moment in pursuit of her freedom, proving over and over again his loyalty, answering every doubt with declarations of love, and daring her each day to take off her blindfold and enjoy the light.

Each time she called for help he would be there. Each time she felt alone he tightly embraced her to remind her that he was there. Each day she spent with him made her feel more alive and each day that passed he gained a little more of her trust until finally one day she was ready.

It was a day no different from any other day. In fact, it was exceptionally ordinary. But for her this was a day that would change the course of her history. This was the day when she would choose to see the light.

He looked at her, as he always did, with admiration in his eyes. She had grown so much in the time they had spent together. If you were to meet her now you would never guess of her time in the darkness for she was naïvely drenched in glory and her smile beamed with life. Today, as he watched her recklessly running blindly towards him, he knew she was ready.

He ran to meet her and caught her mid stumble. They laughed as they collided, elation tangled between them. A beautiful paradox of chaos and order.

"I have something exciting to tell you!" she panted out of breath.

"Oh, what's that?" he asked pretending not to know, excitement sparkling in his eyes.

"I'm finally ready," she exclaimed with joy, "I'm ready for you to take off my blindfold!"

He smiled brightly. "I can't wait for you to experience the light!"

She wrapped her arms tightly around him and buried her face in his chest. "Ok, let's get this over with," she said a little fear trembling in her voice muffled by his embrace.

He squeezed her tightly and kissed her forehead sweetly. Then he reached up and began to slowly untie her blindfold. He could feel her trembling against him and she squeezed him tighter with each tug of the blindfold as it came unraveled. He whispered comforting words softly in her ear as he went.

"I love you, dear one."
"You are greater than your darkness."
"You are strong."
"You are not alone."

Peace overtook her more and more with every word he uttered and before she knew it the blindfold had been completely removed and her eyes were once again overwhelmed by the light.

He reached down and held her hands tightly, "Don't be afraid, I'm right here with you."

His presence gave her strength and the more she abandoned resistance to the light the more pleasant it became to her. How often it is that the moment the fight is forsaken is the same moment that it is won. When she had surrendered all control it was then that she began to see the beauty that was around her.

Splendor entranced her eyes, wonders of which she had never dreamed came into focus, and she opened her eyes wide trying her best to take it all in. Vibrant color burst around her and her jaw dropped open as she was left speechless by the magnificence of it.

"I can't believe... I just... you... you were right all along," she managed to stammer out struggling to find words. With that she turned to catch a glimpse of him for the first time.

She was shocked to see that he looked not unlike her. His hair was tussled and uncombed and his clothes worn and tattered. His tennis shoes caked with dust from his journey and cracking at the soles. His hands were rough and calloused as you would expect those of a laborer to be. He looked at her with a gleam of fondness glistening from his dark brown eyes that she caught herself getting lost in.

He nodded toward the world around her. "It's beautiful isn't it? This is what my world looks like, and I'm giving it to you so that you never again have to be bound by darkness."

"Why... why would you give this to me? Knowing who I am, where I come from, what I deserve, how could you lavish such beauty on messy, dirty me?" she inquired still having trouble forming words.

His eyes were filled with sincerity and he answered her gently. "Because I love you. Because the light does not operate as the darkness does. Light gives when darkness takes. Light provides when darkness demands. Light exposes when darkness hides. Light stands fearless when darkness trembles in terror. Light is relentless when darkness quits. I lavish on you because I am light and that is what light does."

She fell to her knees as she had done when light first came in to her world. This time her sobs were not of fear but of gratitude. He knelt down and gently wiped a tear from her cheek.

"You are now forever a child of the light, bearing my name and a royal birthright. Darkness will try again to bring shadows to your world, but it no longer has power here. Do not let it frighten you into putting your blindfold back on."

"But... what if I fail?" she asked timidly.

"Well then, you need only ask and I will take if off again for you." She looked up to see his eyes still shining with love, squinted by the smile affixed to his face. "Don't worry about failing, just enjoy the light!" he encouraged happily.

She smiled up at him and jumped to her feet ready to explore this new life of light. In the days that followed she spent her time with him going on many adventures and enjoying a life painted with hues of brilliance. Times came when she would retreat to her blindfold, but each time she did he was there with whispers of love and a gentle touch to remove it. Though she didn't always do everything perfectly, she was flawless in his eyes. Soon after much patient persisting from him, she agreed to join him on his journey where she delighted in bringing light to others caged by darkness.

Thus is the story of the man of the light, who came into darkness and was not overcome by it. In him was life and his life brought light to all those he crashed into so that children of darkness might be adopted into the light and reign as royalty by his side for ages to come. May you be lucky enough to have him run into you and when he does, may you be brave enough to let him take off your blindfold.

THE RAGAMUFFIN ROYAL

A parable of addiction and adoption

"Getting sober never felt like I had pulled myself up by my own spiritual bootstraps. It felt instead like I was on one path toward destruction and God pulled me off of it by the scruff of my collar, me hopelessly kicking and flailing and saying, 'Screw you. I'll take the destruction please.' God looked at tiny, little red-faced me and said, 'that's adorable,' and then plunked me down on an entirely different path."

-Nadia Boltz-Webber

"To live by grace means to acknowledge my whole life story, the light side and the dark. In admitting my shadow side I learn who I am and what God's grace means."

-Brennan Manning

The town was quiet as midnight's darkness stilled the streets. The only light that could be seen was that of the small rays that sneaked under door frames. The air was crisp and damp and left those caught in it with a tingle down their spines. The beautiful architecture of buildings looked haunting in the dark, seeming to stretch higher against the background of speckled stars.

It was a nice town, a quiet town. It was ruled by a wise and kind king who took a very hands-on approach to ruling and was found more often in the homes of his people than in his castle at the top of the hill. During the day the city was filled with the hustle and bustle of life. The shrill laughter of children playing filled the air, men and women worked contentedly in their given trades, and old bird dogs stretched out lazily on porches under the warmth of the sun. Here people had their needs met and lived in satisfaction at the hands of their king. Here only pleasant things happened in the light.

What happened in the dark, however, was a different story all together. Between the well-kept buildings down the dark labyrinth of alleyways, all felt the seedy slither of the Dark Man. Here in the shadows pleasantries were nowhere to be found. Here there was only want, desperate and unquenchable want.

This was her world or, at least, the only one she had ever known. Her mother was a cruel and callous woman, a harlot, who made what little money they had by servicing the more lustful residents of the town and peddling elixirs for the Dark Man (who was rarely one to do the dirty work himself). Her father was a client, which one no one knew, and she reasoned she was better for not knowing. Her mother had fallen victim long ago to the cold and unforgiving life of the streets, withering to dust unmourned, and leaving her daughter to the only life she had ever known: pain, darkness, addiction. Most of the time she was submissive to this existence, but every so often on clear nights like this one she would look with longing up at the stars and ache for satisfaction.

A chill crept up her spine and the familiar pangs of hunger assailed her. This was not a hunger for bread or for water or for any normal sustenance, but a hunger for the one thing that dulled the sting of life in the shadows-- the Dark Man's elixir. The first time she tasted this enticing substance it brought with it the swoops and swirls of all forms of pleasure. It took her to the highest of highs and made her feel as if she could conquer the world. She was swept away in its sweetness. This was a sweetness she hadn't tasted in a while for it seemed that no matter how much or how often she glugged down the elixir she could never again recapture the high of the first time. And so she found herself needing more and more and still more until she could scarcely go a few hours without craving it and the Dark Man was all but too willing to offer it to her for the more she partook of it the more obligated to him she became. Here she lived, bound to her desires and indebted to the Dark Man.

But tonight she stared at the stars and 5 hours ticked by with her quieting the cravings. Of course, that didn't go unnoticed for very long.

"Well hello my darling!" cooed the Dark Man slipping from the shadows.

The Dark Man was a handsome man, well dressed and well kept. He wore an expensive tailored suit with a silk tie, a small pin in the shape of a cross was fastened to his lapel, and golden cuff links that shimmered when they caught the light. He had a strong jaw, blonde hair that was wavy and well groomed, and sparkling blue eyes that had wooed many. He looked nothing like what you would expect the keeper of the darkness to look like; in fact, he looked exactly like the majority of those living happily in the light. She couldn't explain why but when he was near her she felt an odd mixture of hatred and infatuation and she found herself inexplicably drawn to his presence despite how despicable she found him to be. Tonight, however, she was not happy to see him.

"Save your flattery," she shot back at him coldly.

"Well, *someone* is in a bad mood tonight!" he answered snidely. "I imagine you must be thirsty. You know, all you have to do is ask, Darling. I always have plenty of elixir on tap especially for my favorite customers." A greasy smile masked the counterfeit kindness in his words.

"I don't want any." There was a tremble in her voice that exposed the irresoluteness of her statement.

"Hmmm you don't sound very sure about that? Why are you resisting something that makes you feel so good? Don't you want to feel good?" he asked her, faking concern.

"It doesn't work anymore. I never feel good anymore... not really." Her tone was mixed with sorrow and apathy as she pulled her knees to her chest and sat sloped against the concrete of a building.

"Have it your way then," he hissed revealing his true nature, "but don't forget you still have a hefty debt to pay so don't go getting any ideas that you're actually free." And with those words he slinked back into the darkness to collect from another poor sap who was foolish enough to trust him.

She buried her face into her knees and repeatedly punched the ground until the rough cement tore through her knuckles leaving them bloody and ragged. The sharp pain shooting through her hand provided a temporary reprieve from the increasing agony of withdrawals. Tears made white streaks as they carved out a path down her grime covered cheeks.

"You know, you're going to hurt yourself if you keep that up," said a soft voice from somewhere in the shadows.

Her head shot up and darted back and forth as she tried to determine where the voice was coming from. The voice was unfamiliar to her. "Who's there?" she questioned the darkness angrily, "Show yourself!"

Footsteps made their way towards her and she squinted to make out the figure nearing the beams of moonlight sidling between the buildings in front of her. A rugged looking man with tousled hair and worn clothing appeared in the patch of light at her feet. Vibrant and swirling pictures were drawn across his arms that were left exposed by his dirt stained tank top. She stared up at him wide eyed.

"Here, let me help," he said as he pulled a less than spotless bandana out of his back pocket wrapping it around her bleeding knuckles.

She pulled her hand back quickly. "What do you care?"

Well, I'd rather you not be in pain, and I'd like to help where I can with that," he answered her hostility with gentleness and seemed unaffected by the harsh tone in her voice.

She laughed at the audacity of it. "You don't even know me."

"I'd like to." His smile sparkled with sincerity.

She looked at him in confusion. "You must not be from around here," she said matter-of-factly as she turned her back and began to walk back home.

"What gave me away?" He laughed following behind her.

"You're too kind for the streets. You'll get yourself hurt out here if you keep that up for much longer."

"Oh don't worry about me, I think I can handle myself," he answered confidently.

Hmph. She snorted doubtfully. "It's your funeral."

She whipped around quickly and shoved the palm of her hand squarely in the middle of his chest. "Did I say you could follow me?"

"Awe come on, give me a chance at least, I just wanna talk, get to know you a little, like you said I'm not from around here and you seem to know these streets pretty well." He pleaded with her.

She looked him up and down trying to decide what to do. He could be the distraction she needed to keep her from the elixir. But could she trust him? He came out of nowhere, she'd never seen him before, and she knew everyone on these streets. Could he be one of the Dark Man's minions and this was just another cruel and sadistic trick to make her even more indebted to him? No... no, he was different. He was different in a way that she couldn't figure out or explain. There was something about his essence that evoked security and brought a different kind of calamity to her comfortable chaos. Emptiness once again clawed at her insides. Seven hours now since her last drink. What's the worst that could happen? She had nothing left. Death? Could that be it? What was death if not escape from this life of drought and degradation? Very well then, she had made her decision.

"Fine. But you're not following me home. Come back tomorrow, we'll meet back where we first met tonight and go from there."

"Deal! Don't forget about me!" he said smiling as he disappeared into the darkness.

Sleeplessness. Craving. Pain. Struggle. Failure.

Her night was not an easy one. As the light peeked through the makeshift walls of her cardboard and canvas home she came down off her elixir fueled high and crashed into the devastation of her failure to resist its pain numbing charms. She carved another notch into the cement beneath her that was already covered in thousands of them. Another payment she owed the Dark Man.

She forced herself to her feet as a hazy memory of the promise she made the mysterious man in the shadows urged her back to the place where they had first met. He was waiting for her.

"Hey! You came!" He shouted loudly with genuine excitement in his voice, "I have to admit, I was a little worried you wouldn't show."

She groaned as the shrill sounds of his joy irritated her already pounding headache. "Ok, first of all, yelling? Not necessary. Secondly, no one should be *that* excited this early in the morning. Are you sure you're human?" Her tone told him that she was annoyed.

He thought for a minute, pinched his arm, and shrugged his shoulders. "Last time I checked!" he answered with a smirk and a playful wink.

She rolled her eyes.

"Come on, don't be mad at me! Look, I even brought breakfast." With that he tossed her a fresh banana.

She looked down in wonder at the bright yellow fruit in her hands. She hadn't seen fresh fruit in years. Her mouth watered at the sight of it, and much to her chagrin, the grumble in her stomach revealed her gratitude.

"Where did you get this?" she wondered.

"I brought it from home," he answered casually. "I thought you might need a little something. You seemed a little worse for wear last night."

"I can take care of myself." She retorted forcefully, feeling exposed.

"Hmm. Yeah, I can see that," he said doubtfully, eyeing her shaking hands and strung out twitches.

"I don't need your charity," she said tossing the banana back to him. She turned to walk away suddenly coming to her senses that maybe hanging around this mystery stranger wasn't such a great idea after all.

"Wait!" He called after her, "How about we make a deal then?"

She turned around. "What kind of deal?"

"A trade. You're an elixir junkie, right?" He questioned knowingly.

She was taken aback. Was it that obvious? "Yeah, what do you know about it?" She shot back.

"I'll trade you then. As much food as you can eat each day for one bottle of elixir until you're all out."

It seemed a little too good to be true. Maybe this would even help her complete the desperate desire of her heart—to give up the elixir for good. She would be getting the better end of the deal, but how could he know that? Surely he didn't she reasoned.

"Seems fair enough." She conceded, offering her hand to shake on it.

"Deal!" he said excitedly shaking her hand and giving her the banana.

He was true to his word and each day they met he would bring with him a cart full of food, more even than she could eat, and she would trade him a bottle from her stash of elixirs. With each day that passed she drank less, choosing instead to gorge herself on the fine foods that he gave generously. They soon became good friends, talking and laughing over broken bread and a thermos full of coffee. She taught him of the horrors that life between the buildings brought and he wooed her with tales of day life in the village. He called her beautiful like it was her name, and not in the way that men had once done with her mother. He did it not to win her love but rather to remind her that she was someone worth loving. Their intimacy was more familial than sensual and she imagined this might be what having a brother was like. She became tangled in the pleasure of his company and before she realized it she was out of elixir, a week dry, and a month without a visit from the Dark Man.

Whee, whee, whee-oh

She heard their secret whistle outside the flap of her riff-raff structure. "Come on in if you want!" she shouted out to him.

He lifted up a piece of the canvas and ducked under it. "Good morning, tough girl," he said with a teasing smirk.

"Oh, shut up!" She snorted playfully punching his shoulder.

He sat on the floor near the bundle she called a bed and patted the ground next to him motioning for her to sit down. "I have something I want to talk to you about," he said with a serious tinge to his voice.

She sat next to him, worry in her voice. "What's wrong?"

He smiled at her. That smile, oh that smile, how effortlessly it demolished the well-guarded walls of her heart.

"Nothing's wrong, love, but I have something important I want to ask you."

She listened intently.

"Run away with me," he pleaded, eyes glimmering of sincerity and adoration.

She looked at him confused. "Run away with you? Where?"

"Home. My home. My father is a good man, a kind man. He knows you and we both want you to come and live with us, you know, be part of our family."

Family. Did she really know what that looked like? Her experience with family was of absence, abuse, and abandonment. And did his father really know her, the real her?

"Surely your father must not know me, not really anyway. If he did he would never invite me into your home. Who wants a junkie street rat to be a part of their family? I love you but you are naïve, you think too much of me." Her voice was filled with sorrow and honesty.

"I am not blind. I know exactly who you are and where you come from. I see these canvas walls and your debts notched in your floor. You have been birthed and bred in the struggle of the street. I am offering you a new birthright, a new name, a new life. My father sees you as I do and offers you adoption into our family. Please come with me?" The earnestness and depth of love that sparkled in his eyes was impossible for her to resist. And she didn't want to.

She tried and failed to mask her excitement at the possibility. "Yes! Oh yes I want to be a part of your family, but... the Dark Man... I owe him a great debt and he will not stop pursuing me until he has collected it."

"The Dark Man has no claim on those under my roof," he said sternly, anger burning behind his eyes.

She had never seen him angry before and the fire she heard in his voice made her very sure that he was serious. She grabbed his hand and pulled him to his feet. "Well? What are you waiting for? Let's go!"

He wrapped her in a bone crushing embrace, pulling her out the door and towards town. "I can't wait for you to be home!" he shouted joyfully.

They ran together through the maze of alleyways between the buildings and out towards the hustle and bustle of town. She balked for a moment before her first step out into town. She had never been out of the shadows before. But he gave her hand a comforting squeeze and thus the courage to step out into village life. She squinted as the brilliance of the sun's rays, unobstructed by buildings, hit her eyes for the first time.

The city life was more wonderful than she ever imagined. Street vendors with every sort of sweet bread lined the stone roads meandering through town. Children laughed and played in the grassy knoll in the middle of town. Business owners waved at passersby and everyone happily greeted him as they made their way through town.

Of course he was loved by all, she thought. He was pretty fantastic after all. They walked all the way through town and down an old dirt road that cut through a small forest. "Where do you live?" she asked right as the trees cleared revealing a colossal castle at the top of a hill covered in sunflowers.

He nodded towards it. "There."

Her jaw dropped. She had only heard stories of the king and the glory of his castle. Never would she have imagined looking at it.

"Wait... you mean... you're the prince?" she said aghast.

He smiled at her sheepishly. "Yep, that's me, and soon you will be royalty too!"

She was left speechless, unable to accurately express how overcome she was with emotion. They walked the rest of the way in silence as she clung tightly to his arm for comfort. As they entered the castle doors they were showered with a jubilant welcome. The smells of cooking food struck her nostrils. Her senses were overwhelmed by the sights and sounds and smells of the palace. Then she caught sight of the king who just so happened to be running full speed towards them. She braced herself for rejection. Surely he would come to his senses upon seeing the ragged state of her.

But, come to his senses he did not, for his pace never slowed and he came barreling into them with a tackling embrace that brought them to the ground. "Welcome home, children!" His deep jovial voice echoed off the walls.

"I... can't... breathe..." She choked out, still trapped under his flooring hug.

"Oh, sorry about that," he laughed heartily, "I'm just so excited to have you both home!"

She stared at him bewildered, still too in awe to speak. "We're glad to be home too, dad." He answered for them both with a bright smile.

Before she knew it she had new clothes and had enjoyed a hot bath for the first time ever in her life. To call it paradise would be an understatement. They enjoyed a euphoric feast together as a family and she ate until she couldn't fit another bite into her stomach. There was celebration and merriment and it was all for her homecoming? It was difficult for her to comprehend it all.

The adoption was finalized only a few days later. She was officially a princess. She enjoyed the royal life and all the pleasures it had to offer. She was never in want. Never hungry or cold or tired. She went on long walks through the garden with the king and enjoyed picnics with the prince in the sunflower field near the castle. This was ecstasy and yet... still lingering in the back of her being was a constant tickle of fear that one day the Dark Man would show up to collect her debt.

Though he tried desperately to convince her otherwise the fear persisted and she found that the more she focused on this fear the less satisfied she was by the pleasures of the palace. That's when the cravings started. They were small at first a fleeting thought of how good a drink of elixir would taste, quickly shooed away as she distracted herself with some royal action or another. Soon though what was once a whisper became a deafening gong in her mind that she could no longer silence. Fear had stolen her focus.

Shame came next to steal her confidence. Guilt plagued her. What would the king think of her if he knew her struggle? Surely THEN he would disown her as she had worried from the beginning. What would the prince say if he knew she was still held tightly in the grip of the Dark Man? He would be heartbroken and she couldn't face that.

The past came last to steal her security. *I am worthless. I am homeless. I am dirty. I don't belong here.* She thought to herself. And with that last theft she was left emotionally bankrupt, deciding secretly it was time for her to run away. It was just better that way. She needed to get herself together before she could be here. She needed to fix herself first so she didn't hurt these wonderful people that she loved so much. And so she ran.

It was dark when she left, all was quite in the castle. She ran as fast and as far as she could. It wasn't long before the first glimmers of light began to sneak over the horizon. The wind blew the tears that cascaded down her cheeks back into her face as she ran and ran until finally she collapsed from exhaustion in the middle of a large wooded area miles from the castle. She wept bitterly, desperate to be rid of the hurt.

As she wiped the tears away from her swollen eyes she caught a glimpse of a small wooden house not far in the distance. Atop the roof was a bright white cross that sparkled in the sunlight. She knew of these buildings from books she had read in the palace library. They were known as refuges for weary travelers and were rumored to hold the answers to life's most pressing questions. A trace of hope flickered within her. She pulled herself to her feet and walked toward it.

Arriving quickly, she swung open the large creaking wooden doors and walked inside. The atmosphere was quiet and reverent. A few people were scattered amongst the pews, some sobbing quietly, others reading from a hard back book, and a few meditating silently in the back. None of them seemed to notice her.

"I'm looking for someone to talk to," she said somewhat loudly.

One parishioner pointed to a man in the corner with his back turned towards her. She walked over to him and patted him on the shoulder to get his attention. What she saw when he turned around made her gasp in anxious shock.

"Well, well, look who we have here!" tutted the Dark Man.

"Wha-- what are you doing here?" she stammered out, "Aren't these places supposed to be a safe place for people in trouble?"

"Ah yes, my dear, well what better place for me to be then? These are ripe hunting grounds for those in search of a temporary fix. Wanna know the best part? These fools actually think what I offer them is righteous and good! They are worse off than even you, darling, for they are indebted to me without even knowing and for those who discover their debt I simply convince them that it's the king who will come to collect and not I. It's my best work yet!" He laughed a noxious and grimy laugh, winking at her, extremely pleased with himself.

She was disgusted by him. Why couldn't she be free from his filth?

"So... have you come to pay your debt or to get a fix?" he questioned her.

"I cannot pay," she said with sorrow.

"A fix then?" He was more than happy to offer it to her.

"Yes… a fix." She conceded to the fate she had feared for so long.

He tossed her a bottle of elixir and scooted her out the door. "Go on now, you'll ruin the con if they see me with the likes of you!"

She was devastated and so she did what she always did, she wrapped her lips around the bottle and pulled the trigger to kill another piece of her soul. Days she spent strung out on the numbing liquid, somehow finding her way back to the schlocky corner of the shadows that she had once called home. She resigned to her pathetic existence here.

Days went by, weeks, and she lost count of the time for she was too intoxicated to know day from night and too disoriented to care about either. One night she was awakened from her drunken slumber by a firm hand shaking her forcefully.

"Wake up!" said a familiar voice.

She rubbed the sleep from her eyes trying her best to focus through the blurred lens of elixir. For the first time in weeks she saw the familiar tattooed hands of her prince grabbing her arms.

"What? Why are you here?" she managed to slur out.

"I'm here to get you and bring you home. You don't belong here!" he insisted.

"Ha! Oh silly boy, don't you see now?" She laughed tipsy and uninhibited. "This is where I belong. I can never pay my debt to the Dark Man and as long as that is true I will always end up back here."

"Did he tell you that?" he questioned angrily.

"What's it matter? It's the truth. Go on now! Get out of here! Go back to your castle that's where you belong!" she screamed at him.

"I'll go for now," he conceded, "But I'll be back for you. I promise."

With that he disappeared into the dark and she snorted in dejected disbelief of his promise. Now he had seen the real her. He wouldn't be back for that horrid creature. But she was wrong. Three days later she did, in fact, see him again.

It was late evening and she was briefly sober as she walked the streets foraging for scraps of food before returning to suckle at the teat of her habit. She came to the spot where she had first met the tattooed prince with calloused hands. A tinge of regret stabbed her heart. If only it could have been real.

Then, all of a sudden, she heard a faint groan coming from the shadows near the building. At first she ignored it, but the harder she listened the more it sounded like whimpers of pain and she was moved with compassion. She walked gingerly over to the spot the sound was coming from.

She was gripped with anger and sorrow at what she found there. It was none other than her prince, bloodied, beaten, and barely breathing. She pulled his tattered body into her arms as she held back tears feigning strength.

"What happened to you?!" she demanded with concern.

"I..." He gasped for breath and she leaned in close so she could hear his answer. "I paid your debt," he pushed out barely above a whisper.

She looked at him in horror and disbelief. "You did what?!" she shouted.

"Your debt to the dark man is paid. It's finished. I made a deal with the Dark Man- My blood for your freedom. No matter what you do, how much elixir you come looking for, you will never again owe him anything. That's the deal. See, you don't belong here," he said softly, a small smile curling across his bloodied lip.

She pulled him to her chest, tears streaming down her face. "You didn't have to do that. Don't you see what a mess I am? There are those far more deserving of having their debts settled."

"I did. I did have to do that. You are worth that. I don't care what you think about yourself. I did it because of my love for you, not the other way around."

She shook her head in utter amazement at the depth of his sacrifice. "How can I ever repay you?"

"You don't owe me anything. You are free."

She squeezed him tightly. She looked upon him with awe and wonder, her heart bursting with more love than she had ever believed she could feel, and she knew that she never again wanted to live life apart from him.

"Hey, Sis," he whispered.

"Yeah?"

"Can we go home now?" he begged.

She smiled at him sweetly and helped him to his feet. She threw his arm over her shoulder and together they made the long trek back to the castle. When they arrived they were met with concern and his wounds were immediately attended to. Some worry bubbled in her stomach at the thought of facing the king but when he saw her he rushed to her, wrapped her in a warm embrace, and kissed her forehead sweetly.

"I'm so glad you're home safe," he said with a sigh of relief.

She looked up at him with gratefulness that was beyond words, buried her head in his chest, and sobbed. He comforted her and held her tight and for the first time in her life she felt like she truly belonged to a family.

One might consider this a good place to end her story. All things having been completed and resolved, all struggles conquered. But that's not how her story ends.

Though she was at rest, home at last, her struggle did not magically disappear simply because her debt had been paid. She had spent almost 20 years of her life in the gutter, need and want clawing at her soul. The transition to fullness and rest was a difficult one. There were times when she would run back to the alley and each time she did the prince would come and take her by the hand and lead her home.

She always willingly returned with him for deep in her being she knew that she no longer belonged there. Her times of flight got fewer and her craving for that which left her empty became quieter but they did not cease completely.

More faithful though than her cravings was the love of the king and his son, her royal family. Never once did they falter in gracious outpouring of love and acceptance. Where she was need they were source, and an unending one. Never once did the prince tire of pursuing her. Never once did the king give thought to disowning her. She was bought by royal blood and with it forever sealed as a daughter of the king.

Today you will find her walking through town with her brother, the tattooed prince. The last time she ran towards the door she came to a dead stop in the threshold as she heard the tender call of her father from his studio, "Oh good, you're awake, come and create with me!" It has been 8 years since her last retreat into darkness. The battle still rages within her but never again will it rise to steal her birthright.

The Dark Man has no claim on children of the king.

THE WARRIOR AND THE MOUNTAIN MAN

A parable of fear and faith

"How bold one gets when one is sure of being loved."

-Sigmund Freud

"Trust him. And when you have done that, you are living the life of grace. No matter what happens to you in the course of that trusting - no matter how many waverings you may have, no matter how many suspicions that you have bought a poke with no pig in it, no matter how much heaviness and sadness your lapses, vices, indispositions, and bratty whining may cause you - you believe simply that Somebody Else, by his death and resurrection, has made it all right, and you just say thank you and shut up."

-Robert Capon

She weaved her way between the trees, running frantically, her breath shallow and rapid matching the beat of her heart that was quickened by fear. She dare not look back for she was sure that if she did it would catch her. The cracking of the branches behind her warned her it was getting closer, her chest was heavy and tight from exhaustion; she had been running for so long now.

To know her you would be puzzled to see her like this... running away. Where she lived she was known as a warrior, fearlessly facing war as it raged towards her. She was the defender of the weak, the strength of the weary, and the refuge for the frightened. There she was honored, revered, and respected; here she was alone, forsaken, and terrified. How disappointed they would be if they could see her now. After all, no one wants to believe that their warriors are vulnerable underneath their armor. Even heroes fall and the bravest of soldiers have monsters under their beds. So here she was, running in terror from her monster.

Its existence was no surprise to her, she had known of it for some time now. She had locked it away many years ago, hoping to never again have to face it. There were times when it would bang loudly against its bars or reach between them trying to grab her, but it had never escaped before. Until now that is.

How could I have been so careless?! She thought to herself as she coaxed the last bit of energy into her legs and sped up.

Soon she came to the end of the woods and as she pushed her way through the last of the trees her heart fell into her stomach and panic overcame her. In front of her stood a mountain that stretched so high clouds hid the top of it. She looked desperately for a way around it but found that it was as wide as it was tall. She fell hopelessly to her knees, her legs finally surrendering to exhaustion. What would she do now? Any minute now her pursuer would be upon her and in front of her stood an immovable wall of rock. Would this be how things would end for her?

She sat there, panting heavily as her heart worked hard to regulate itself, and she resigned to her fate. Then suddenly, she heard what sounded like a voice.

PSSSSSST!

She whipped her head around to face the noise. It seemed to be coming from inside the mountain. She squinted her eyes trying to see who might be making it.

"Hey! Over here! I have a safe place you can hide!" beckoned a mysterious male voice.

She had no time to waste worrying whether or not she could trust him; she had to get somewhere safe and fast for she could hear the carnage from the forest nearing her. She willed her legs into one last burst of vigor and darted towards the voice.

She burst through a grouping of branches near the base of the mountain and tumbled headfirst into the mouth of a small, well-hidden cave carved into the side of it. Two strong arms pulled her into safety and the mouth of the cave disappeared before her very eyes like magic. *What kind of sorcery was this?* She wondered this to herself as a tickle of fear moved across her stomach. She pushed the feeling aside aware that she had no choice but to believe this was a safe place. Her eyes darted back and forth taking in the scene around her.

It was nothing like you'd expect from a cave. It wasn't musty or dirty. Light bounced off the walls and shadows fled from it. There was a large table with any kind of food you could imagine covering it. Music echoed softly though the caverns and she felt a sudden wave of peace sweep over her. She stared in amazement.

Suddenly a large bottle of water appeared in front of her face and caused her to cross her eyes as she tried to focus on it. "Here, drink this," said the voice, and she realized a hand with colorful markings across it was gripping the bottle. Her eyes followed the hand up an equally colorful arm that was muscular and unrestricted by sleeves, across a well-built chest, until they finally landed on a handsome face covered in a scruffy beard.

She grabbed the water and slurped it down greedily but did not take her eyes off of him. When she had finished her last gulp she questioned him, "Who are you? What is this place?"

"A friend. This is my place of rest for those who are weary. It's pretty cool, huh? I designed it myself!" His answer was full of joy and life and the smile on his face grew as he spoke.

She ogled him, staring deeply into his eyes. She couldn't help herself, there was just something mesmerizing about them. They were a deep dark chocolate brown that glinted with glory and seemed a stark contrast to the almost unbearable brightness of his smile.

"Are you hungry?" His question jerked her back into reality. She nodded furiously, famished from her flight.

"Take all you like," he said nodding towards the large banquet table adorned with food across the room.

She ran to the table immediately, her eyes widening with hunger, and began to shovel food into her mouth without any thought to how sloppy she must have looked to him. He, however, didn't seem to notice how messy she was. Instead he looked at her affectionately, eyes sparkling with love, and delighted himself in giving her all she asked for. After some time she leaned back in her chair and gave a satisfied sigh, her belly full and her muscles refreshed.

She looked up from the table to see him building a fire in the corner of the cave. She walked over to him and began to pick up some branches from his pile, "Here, I can help, it's the least I could repay you for you kindness!"

He smiled at her, "No please don't, let me handle the work, you just sit here and rest, you're weary."

She couldn't argue with him because... well, because he was right. "How... how long can I stay here?" she asked him timidly.

"You are always welcome here for as long as you need to stay." He answered her softly, compassion dripping from his voice.

"Forever then?" She shot back with a snarky tinge in her voice.

He chuckled, "For as long as you need to stay."

Days went by and she spent every moment with him in the cave. They would laugh and talk and she would tell stories of her great warrior feats and he would listen to her, captivated and proud, cheering and clapping at the end of every one. He would tell her stories too. Stories not of great battles or mighty conquests but of small shepherd boys and grime covered fishermen and she would listen more intently with each story, in constant awe of their great insignificance and their great power. He spoke of love and acceptance, community and connection, vulnerability and authenticity, and in these times she would sit silently listening trying each day to convince herself that such things existed. Each day she became more aware of how much he cared for her and each day she found herself trusting him a little more.

Days turned into weeks, weeks into months, and months into years. Soon she had begun to forget what life outside the cave looked like. Some days she would walk towards the mouth of the cave, but as the tips of her toes began to cross the entrance she would quickly pull her foot back as an itch of panic squirmed in her stomach. *What if that monster is still out there?* She thought, quickly turning around and retreating to the safety of the cave.

One day as they sat telling stories, he asked her a question. He asked her the question that she had dreaded him asking since she arrived.

"Well, you have told me every story of your great and valiant acts as a warrior. I have listened in wonder and excitement as you recounted your great victories. It seems there is only one story left you have yet to tell me, the story of the day you came here. Why were you running?" His voice was kind and soft as it always was.

"I don't want to talk about that," she answered sharply. Her voice was strong and hard as it always was.

"Please, sweetheart? I really want to hear it." He pleaded with her tenderly, his eyes glimmering with concern.

"I... I can't tell you that story," she said looking down at the floor.

"Why not?"

"Because... you will be disappointed with me. It's not a story of victory, it's a story of defeat. You will be ashamed to have called me a warrior, to have loved me, if you knew that story." Her voice shuddered with shame.

He shook his head, gently lifting her chin so he could look her in the eyes, "Silly girl, don't you know? There is nothing you could ever do to make me love you less."

"But..." she started to protest.

"Nothing." he said sternly and resolutely.

Just as on the day she had first caught a glimpse of them, she found herself lost in his eyes, overwhelmed by the depth and breadth and height of his love for her. She half smiled at him, one lone tear escaping from the corner of her eye. So she told him her story. A story that she had not told anyone before. One that, in some ways, she had not even let herself think about entirely.

She told him of the first time the monster had become a part of her life, loosed upon her by someone she loved. It was a time when she was young and weak, defenseless against its savagery. She lifted her shirt to show him the scars still left carved into the skin of her innocence. Tears welled in his eyes. She told him of her escape from that place of anguish, held captive by her monster. She told of her flight to a new land with new people, where no one knew of her monster. There she made a new life and what were once bleeding wounds turned into scars that she hid expertly beneath her armor. She hardened her heart and sharpened her sword, determined never again to be a victim. And she fought, war after war, battle after battle, defending the weak, rescuing the wounded, and championing the voiceless. All the while she knew the monster was still out there, and she lived in fear of it.

She went on to tell him of when it found her again. This time she was ready, armed and equipped for battle. This time she fought back and was able to capture it. She locked it away deep in the darkness where she dare not visit, for terror still overtook her in its presence. Finally she told of its escape from her captivity and of her panicked exodus to the forest. She spoke of how weary she was of running away, and of how she craved desperately to be free from its torture. He looked at her empathetically and she wept.

When she managed to finally quiet her crying she wiped the remnants of tears from her eyes with the back of her hand and said, "See, I told you that you'd be disappointed. Now you know, I'm no warrior. I am weak."

At that he pulled her mightily into his arms and squeezed her tightly. "You are stronger than you know and braver than you believe. I know no truer warrior than you." His voice was soft and sweet and it wrapped around her cocooning her in comfort. She had never been so known and so loved.

"Do you really want to be free from this monster?" he inquired.

"Of course I do!" she answered strongly thinking it was a somewhat stupid question.

"I can help you with that, but you will have to trust me," he answered, aware of but unoffended by her thought.

"I trust you... most days..." she chuckled honestly.

"If you truly wish to be free you will have to trust me completely. You will have to trust that I am for you and your freedom and that everything I do will be for both of those things. You will have to trust that everything I do will be what is best for you, that everything I do, I do because I love you. Can you do that?"

She thought back on the years she had spent with him, how glorious they had been. She remember the care and affection he had showered on her in every moment. She recalled his constant patience and kindness in the midst of her aggression and abrasiveness. She looked in his eyes once more and confidence welled in her soul.

"Yes. I can do that," she answered assertively.

He smiled at her enthusiastically, "Well then, let's show this monster who's boss!"

He began to teach her not how to kill the monster (which is what she had expected) but rather how to tame the monster. At first she didn't understand this, "Why don't we just kill it?" she asked him.

"Everyone has monsters. Some are big and some are small. Some come out only at night and some hide in familiar places. Some are loud and demanding and others are quiet and sneaky.

It's not the existence of monsters that creates chaos but the fear of them. You could kill your monster, if you wish, but your fear would not die with it and soon a new monster would come to take its place."

For the first time in her life she felt like someone else truly understood what living with a monster felt like and from that moment on she did not question him. In the days that followed she learned much from him, but most importantly she learned how to overcome her fear. She grew in confidence and strength and soon she was ready to once again leave the cave and face her monster.

As she stepped across the threshold her hands trembled like leaves shaken from trees by the chill of a winter wind. Choppy seas of worry made waves in her stomach as anxiety tied sailor knots in her throat to keep her nerve from capsizing beneath them. She took a deep breath, closed her eyes, and braced herself for the ominous entity that quickly approached her.

The rumble of a sinister growl made the ground beneath her feet shake as if it too were trying to run and hide. A hot and rancid breath fell on her face and she opened her eyes to see a pair of menacing eyes glaring back at her. Hairy drool covered lips pulled into an evil smirk offering her a brief reprieve from the two intimidating rows of sharp teeth that hid behind it.

Her first inclination was to run but at the very moment she was about to move her feet for the first step, a strong hand rested reassuringly on her shoulder. It was the familiar gentle touch of a cave man and immediately her boldness was restored. She stood powerfully and creased her brow purposefully.

"I'm... I'm not afraid of you!" She managed to squeak out, still trying to untangle the knots in her throat.

A deafening roar of laugher shook the earth followed by a snort of disbelief. The beast wasn't buying it. She stood up straighter and clenched her fists tightly.

"I. Am Not. Afraid of you." This time her voice rang of poise and valor burned in her eyes. "You have no power over me anymore!"

The monster took a surprised step backward then raised a massive arm covered in sharp claws above its head preparing to attack. The man of the mountain stepped in front of her ready to take the blow. At the sight of him, the beast retreated whimpering. She smiled victoriously walking confidently towards the cowering creature.

"You will no longer be my master. You will not make me run and you will not hurt me." She said this with a strength that had long been hidden in her. The monster yielded its will and the man looked on with joy and pride.

Things were never the same after that day. When war arose the warrior rode her monster into battle, stronger than ever against the forces that tried to overtake her. She faced her monsters are wore her scars like wings. As for the mountain man, well, he continued to keep his cave ready for those in need of it. She would return quite often to the cave sometimes bringing people with her. She came not to hide but to rest and to tell him stories of her battles both won and lost. He always listened intently for he delighted in her on her best days and on her worst days.

She was a warrior, brave and free. He was a mountain man, kind and caring. She fought for the weak ones and he offered rest for the wounded. Together they taught all they touched the secret to defeating their monsters. What is that secret you ask?

It's simply this: Courage is not the absence of fear. Courage is looking fear dead in the eyes and saying with confidence, "You. Will not. Beat me." May all who hear their story be encouraged to live courageously.

THE SHADOW PEOPLE

A parable of conflict and community

"Grace is even for those who do not understand it, for those even who preach against it. This seems unfair, but such is the nature of grace."

-Joe Langley

"Grace leaves us anchored not angered."

-Andrew Farley

She sat resolute in a room of indecision and uncertainty. Her brow creased with determination as she glanced around the room. An uproar had recently broken out at the call for decision. Shrill voices pierced the air and clergy clamored for credit as one after another they presented their "life changing ideas" to the prim and proper postured that filled the pews.

The latter nodded in agreement with each argument; a hearty "Amen" escaping the lips of a pot-bellied man in the second row every now and then. She sat silently in the back observing the occurrences of the morning. Some shot sideways glances her way; her position was not a secret. Shaking her head she told herself it was time to go. Suddenly, a man sat down next to her.

"Damn it. What are you doing here?" She questioned the man sternly.

"What? You were saving this seat for someone else?" he asked sarcastically, shooting her a wink and a smug smile.

She sighed and slouched back in the pew, crossing her arms defiantly. "Actually, I was just leaving so..."

"No, stay, this is important!" he implored her.

"Right, people yelling, super important," she said cynically.

"Come on, for me?" He looked at her sweetly, pushing out his bottom lip childishly.

She rolled her eyes, "Fiiiiiiine!"

SHHHHHH!

She looked up to see a red-faced woman shushing them from the row in front of where they were seated.

"Oh, sorry about that!" he apologized.

She stuck her tongue out at the back of the woman's head.

"Why do you want me to stay anyway?" She questioned him sassily.

"You'll see," he answered softly.

About that time a stern voice silenced the room. "Listen," said a man who looked to be in charge, "we simply can't go on this way. Look how empty these seats are, and more importantly my job is on the line here!"

She rolled her eyes, her lips pursed in anger. She was so tired of hearing about his needs, his wants, and his passions. How dare she care about anything else? How dare she fan the flames of revolution in *his* church? Dare indeed she did for she had a heart like black powder and hands that played fearlessly with matches. Explosion… explosion happened and for that she refused to apologize.

"It's sad isn't it?" The man next to her questioned, his voice ringing of sorrow and sincerity.

"What?" she asked harshly, "the fact that he's a self-righteous ass who's getting what he deserves?" She didn't risk looking him in the eyes as the poisonous words left her lips, for she knew the sadness she would see there would make her regret saying them.

"I guess that means you don't see them then?" His tone was not one of scolding but of empathy.

She looked around confused. "See who? These irate pompous people?"

He chuckled a little but there was no joy in his laugh. "No... the others. Look closer."

Her eyes darted around the room as she strained to see who he could be talking about. She saw gossipy women looking judgmentally out of the corner of their eyes. She saw teenagers with arms insolently folded as time ticked away and brought them closer to their escape. She saw salesmen with slick words making notes for their next pitch. She saw people of all different sorts, but mostly she saw stiff necks and hard hearts and bitter regrets.

"I don't understand," she wondered confused, "What others do you mean?"

"Just wait and watch. You will see soon." There was seriousness in his eyes that she rarely saw. They usually sparkled brightly with life and laughter, but today the glimmer was dulled. The smile that seemed larger each time they encountered one another no longer hung on his face, instead lines of sadness sneaked from the corners of his mouth. She worried what could possibly be hiding out of sight that would cause this man of joy such sorrow.

She waited anxiously, her foot bouncing as she squirmed in her chair, drumming her fingers against her leg. He placed his hand comfortingly on her arm and though he didn't say a word, when she looked up at him it was as if he had spoken the most eloquent and calming of phrases for she felt instantly at ease. And she wondered for the hundredth time why someone like him would hang around with someone like her.

Time passed far too slowly for her liking, men spoke, women cried, somberness suffocated the last bit of authenticity that had managed to survive this long, and after tension had become king people shuffled quickly out the door pretending nothing was wrong. She would never understand how easily the masquerade came to them. After everyone had shuffled out she stood up to leave but he grabbed her arm.

"Now look," he urged her.

"Why? Everyone's gone," she said her voice dripping with defiance.

"Not everyone," he replied softly nodding his head towards the shadows.

She walked towards the dimly lit corner focusing her eyes intently ahead of her. As she got closer, outlines of figures came into view and faint sobs landed on her ears. Her eyes adjusted quickly to the darkness and she was shocked by what she saw. At least twenty people, all looked extraordinarily crestfallen, with tears staining most of their cheeks. The scene was not unlike that of triage after a battle; their sprits bleeding internally from less obvious wounds.

He walked up and stood beside her. "Who... who are they?" she asked with burden in her voice.

"They're the shadow people," he answered as he bent down to care for one of the children, "See, while everyone fights and argues over all the things they should do or shouldn't do they are the ones who get hurt. While you get angry and call for revolution they are the ones who are neglected."

She hung her head in shame. *How could I have been so blind?* She condemned herself silently. He put a gentle arm around her and pulled her tightly into an embrace.

"I didn't bring you here to shame you, silly, I brought you here to show you what is important. I brought you here because they need you."

She looked up and scanned the room. So much hurt. How could she do anything?

"That tender heart of yours that you keep so tightly locked away, that's what they need." He said this as if answering her thoughts. "You're the best person I know to help me with them. If I didn't think so I would have brought someone else here."

"But what if I don't think I can do this?" she asked him timidly.

"Well then, that's your choice and of course I would never make you stay, but as for me this is where I will be, here among the shadow people." He answered her and she heard the sincerity and compassion in his voice.

"Alright. I will help you take care of them. I will tend to their wounds and be with them in their loneliness. You can count on me!" she declared with strength echoing in her voice.

He smiled brightly at her. He adored her passion. "That's my girl!" he said proudly, giving her a wink.

"And… what of the others?" she asked, embers of anger still smoldering behind her eyes.

"I imagine they will go on making their plans and wearing their masks, but as for me this is where I will be, here among the shadow people." And with that he hurried off to tend to a moaning woman against the wall across from them.

Time went by and plans were made. People grew and changed while somehow staying the same, a new package for the same contents. No one seemed to miss her much; in fact, most were glad to have her gone. For those who came looking for her all that they found was a note taped to her door that read:

Many make plans and wear masks, but as for me you will find me among the shadow people.

THE WORLD OF SMUDGES

A parable of memory and emotion

"God, give us grace to accept with serenity the things that cannot be changed, courage to change the things which should be changed and the wisdom to distinguish the one from the other."

-The Serenity Prayer

"Suffering, failure, loneliness, sorrow, discouragement, and death will be part of your journey, but the Kingdom of God will conquer all these horrors. No evil can resist grace forever."

-Brennan Manning

What follows is an excerpt from a recently recovered journal belonging to someone known only as "She." Upon reading the journal, it has been discovered that She was a great warrior of The Kingdom appointed with the mission of exploring all the previously unknown edges of her world.

The exploits outlined in this journal are vast and numerous. She explored many new worlds and discovered both places of beauty and of malevolence in her travels. Each record recounts the glory and danger of the new frontiers she walked down and provides all who read them with well outlined information should they decide to visit in the future.

This particular entry entails her notes from her visit to a place known only as "The World of Smudges." Take care to heed her words lest you find yourself getting lost in such a place.

●●●

It's funny how memories work. You can go days, months, years even and remain unbothered by a memory and then one day, all of a sudden, you find yourself overwhelmed by the rush of emotions exploding out of a memory. It's triggered by something as simple as a touch, a smell, seeing a familiar face, and then all at once you're back in that place—the faded greys of a memory.

Sometimes it's a blessing to visit the World of Smudges, but as you can imagine, it's never as clear a place as one would like for it to be. Once you find yourself walking carelessly in it, you can be easily hoodwinked into believing it is reality, forsaking clarity for comfort.

I'm writing this as one well versed in traveling the world of blurred lines, but don't think for a moment that I have never been deceived by its sepia toned hues. More on that later.

Things work differently here. They ebb and flow in the subjectivity of emotion. There's a fluidity in the atmosphere, an identity to this world that lacks resoluteness. This is one reason I warn you to be alert for even the best of us can be fooled into placing belief firmly on that which bends.

You may ask, "How do I navigate such a place?" It's hard to say really since so much of the individual's experience is unique to them, but I am including a few general tips that are true for most who traverse this place frequently.

Tip #1: Question everything.

It is important to take nothing at face value. Be doubtful, ask questions, and never just believe things simply because you see them. This is a world of mirage. Quite often one can be misled towards an oasis to find that it is only a desert. Things that seem so tangibly real here in this place are, in fact, only vapors, and the moment you reach out to take hold of them you will feel them dissolve quickly between your fingers.

This is not to say that all things in this world are illusions. That's the trick really, to discern what is real and what is not, and that is why you are to continue to question. The more you question, the more you doubt what you see in front of you, and the easier it will be for you to know and treasure what is real here. This place is both paradise and purgatory for the dreamer. We must take care to remember both of those truths.

Tip #2: Don't get too attached.

This is a world of enchantment and wonder. One can become easily bewitched by that which seems to satisfy. It is comforting to both remember things as you wish they were and to forget things that you wish weren't. This World of Smudges offers you both of these possibilities tangled in the charms of wistfulness, but it provides no real antidote to the reality of that which has truly happened. It is quite possible for you to fall into a dizzying spell as you are wooed and entranced by the intoxicating stories that are fabricated before you. As you become quite obsessively infatuated with this fairy tale you will find that you are incapable of forsaking this world for the one of definition.

I myself have fallen victim to this rather unpleasant outcome. I was once naïve and unassuming, and I fell too quickly for the seduction of this dusky hazed place. It was not long before I had been lured into the labyrinth of emotion and found myself unable to navigate my way out. I spent many years in wandering there before I was rescued quite valiantly by one who remains unaffected by the temptation of silvery tones. Do not make the same mistake I did. Be alert.

Tip #3: Never stay too long.

This world was never designed for permanent residence. After all, how can a place that is fleeting offer an enduring experience? It is at its very core a transitory world. It is therefore only effective for short visits at a time lest you find yourself being sucked into the black holed abyss that lies at the heart of the labyrinth. Take care to make your visits brief and purposeful.

Tip #4: Never stop coming to visit.

The World of Smudges in and of itself is not an evil one. It is quite simply a tricky and irresolute neighborhood that you must be careful when visiting. It is important, however, that you never stop visiting. Though most of this world is wispy and ethereal there is still much to be learned from it. As you walk along its winding roads you will find the dusty remnants of past journeys. As you run your fingers through the grassy hills you will feel the lingering dew drops of joy from forgotten friendships. Even as you climb the treacherous and formidable cliffs covered in the jagged rocks of your regrettable pain you will discover that you are better for having surmounted them. So, my friends, I cannot stress enough how significant the visit to the neighborhood is just so long as you don't try to build a house on the block.

Tip #5: Never go alone.

As the old adage goes, two are better than one. I have found that it is much more difficult for the more mischievous attributes of this world to distract you if you have a trusted companion with you. Now, I don't recommend traveling with just anyone. Choose your road trip buddy wisely and only journey with one you can trust to keep your focus on things of substance. You both should pack well stocked bags filled to the brim with structure and certainty. These supplies will come in handy if one or both of you wanders off after this world's wavering wonders.

Most importantly, neither of you should travel without the company of a third companion; the one who I mentioned earlier. He is unaffected by this world's charms and remains the only person I have yet to come across that can easily discern fact from fiction here. He is faithful and loyal and will gladly journey with all who invite him (and even those who don't). On that note, you will notice that he is never too far away even if you forget to send him a travel invite.

I do hope that these few tips aid you in your journey through this world. I leave you with these final admonitions to carry with you along your voyage: Be curious in exploration; be confident in truth, and be satisfied apart from this place. Armed with these three things I am sure that your trips will yield only positive results. Travel safely!

-Sha

THE EMPLOYEE OF THE MONTH

A parable of duty and rest

"The movement of grace often happens with our consent, but it never happens on our initiative."

-John Zahl

"Rest is the ultimate humiliation because in order to rest, we must admit we are not necessary, that the world can get along without us, that God's work does not depend on us. Once we understand how unnecessary we are, only then might we find the right reasons to say yes. Only then might we find the right reasons to decide to be with Jesus instead of working for him."

-Mike Yaconelli

Clickity-clack, clickity-clack.

The sound of her fingers hitting the keyboard sounded more like a stampede of horses in the quiet of the empty office. She was always there long before anyone else arrived. It didn't bother her much that the others didn't come in early; in fact, some mornings she found the solitude to be quite enjoyable. She rarely gave it much thought instead working diligently and efficiently completing the tasks of the day.

This year would mark her 13th year with The Company and she was determined that it would be her best year yet. Admittedly, her first 5 years were a bit of a rough patch. What with the excessive misconduct, numerous missed workdays, and all together unprofessional behavior they contained. In the spring of that fifth year she struck up a wonderful new friendship with a man who lived in her building.

He had a somewhat disheveled appearance. His hair was a mess of unruly curls and his stubble covered cheeks were often unshaven. His usual outfit consisted of blue jeans with holes in the knees and a formerly white t-shirt with one too many grease stains to be considered so anymore. He had the heart of a renegade and a smile that beckoned her to freedom. But he was secure and steadfast in nature, which left her in a constant paradox of reckless calm whenever they were together.

They spent many evenings together sipping strong coffee and enjoying invigorating conversation. It was her opinion that bitter espresso always paired well with sweet company. It was from this friendship that she gained stability and confidence out of which naturally emerged diligence and dedication.

She had made strides in the last 8 years with The Company and she had set her sights on the coveted "Employee of the Month" award. To be honest, she had never personally seen anyone win the award but most of the coworkers she knew were imperfect and she reasoned that the really elite employees must have their own office somewhere else in the building. Everyone in the office talked about the award and dreamed of the honor, so she figured it must be very real and very important. She believed in it so much that she was here, at work before the sun, trying desperately to prove her dedication.

Some hours later the rest of the employees began filtering in, all going straight to their cubicles, powering up their computers, and beginning their work.

Clickity-clack, clickity-clack.

Hours ticked by with each key stroke, every eye glued to their respective computer screens, what good little workers they all were. None of them noticed the blatantly out of place presence of an unkempt man in frayed jeans as he walked into the office. Well, except for her that is.

Catching a glimpse of the familiar figure in the corner of her eye she whipped her head around quickly, eyes widening in surprise. Trying not to cause too much commotion, she got up from her desk and ran quickly to him.

"What are you doing here?!" she whispered firmly.

"Wanna go to lunch?" He beckoned her with a gleam of mischief in his eyes, "There's a great burger place down the street, and I hear they make a killer cheesecake!"

She glanced down at her watch, shocked to see it was already 1pm. Usually lunch was a protein bar and cold coffee at her desk, not wanting to miss a chance to impress the Taskmaster and therefore be kicked out of the running for employee of the month. However, a burger did sound good and cheesecake was her favorite. Her stomach gurgled in agreement.

"Well... I really should get back to work..." she said looking back at her desk.

"Come on," he pleaded, "The work will still be there when you get back."

She couldn't resist his wild eyes and goofily pouted lip. "Alright, let's go!" she conceded with counterfeit selflessness.

And just like that he had pulled her into another adventure. This one consisted of weaving in and out of traffic on his motorcycle (while she clenched her jaw, buried her face in his back, and let out a few yelps every so often when they got especially close to the car in front of them), a greasy spoon diner on the wrong side of the tracks (she stayed glued to his side just in case they ran into any especially seedy characters), and finally the best burger she had ever eaten in her life that was piled high with bacon and grilled onions and oozing barbeque sauce. They shared the biggest piece of cheesecake she had ever seen that was drenched in chocolate syrup and fresh strawberries. Before she knew what had happened, she was lost in this moment with him and he delighted in watching her relax.

As with most great adventures, this one was abruptly interrupted as she once again became suddenly aware of her responsibilities.

"Two O'Clock?!" she shouted, staring at her watch in disbelief, "I have to get back to work!"

He sighed. Not a sigh of disappointment or sadness but the sigh of someone who lived his life without a schedule and wished for others to share in such freedom.

"Are you sure? The highway is right down the road. We could just get on it and drive until we run out of gas. You and me, wild and free, adventurers, gypsies, vagabonds!" He tempted her to recklessness and her heart craved to taste of it.

"You know I can't, why do you keep asking?" she answered doggedly to his outlandish offer.

"Because full hearts always hope, my dear, full hearts always hope." He said this giving her a wink and throwing a wad of cash onto the table to pay their bill.

After another heart quickening ride back to the office she dismounted and hurried back inside eager to get back to her computer. She was so eager, in fact, that she almost tackled an older man who was walking out of her building as she was sprinting in. She gave a half-hearted apology, barely looking at his face, and darted back to her desk.

Clickity-clack, clickity-clack

"*Ahem.*" A loud scratchy grunt pierced the silence of her cubicle.

She looked up to see the Taskmaster looking menacingly over the top of his thick-rimmed bifocal glasses. She braced herself in dread, knowing what was coming next.

"And just where have you been?" He questioned her, a smirk of disdain stretching across his face.

"I... uh... well I thought I'd just take a quick lunch break," she stammered out knowing full well it wouldn't be an acceptable answer.

"Hmph. Here I thought you were on a new path, didn't you want to get employee of the month this year, a better position, maybe even your own office?" he asked her.

She nodded, shame hunching her shoulders with the weight of failure.

"Well how do you expect to be trusted with the big things if you can't be faithful in the little things?" He questioned rhetorically, shaking his head in disapproval. With that he walked away leaving her alone to writhe in the wake of his wounding words.

She choked back the tears that began to well up inside her. She was devastated. Were her years of faithfulness not enough? Were her countless mornings arriving before everyone else or her tireless nights leaving after dark not enough? All those times when she chose to do the jobs that no one else wanted simply because they needed to get done, were those not a sign of being faithful in the small things?

No. It seemed perfection and dedication in every moment was required and she feared she might never measure up. Still, she worked until well after all the others had gone home that night.

By the time she got home she was utterly exhausted. She quickly changed from her corporate costume into her favorite skull patterned pajama pants and oversized t-shirt, popped her favorite coffee pod into her brew station, and walked out on to her balcony to enjoy the cool of the night air.

"You're home late," said a familiar voice.

She turned to see him lounging on his favorite chair on his own balcony. She glared at him, pursed her lips, and turned away pretending he wasn't there.

"Rough day then?" he asked unaffected by her anger.

"Yeah. Thanks to you." She grumbled under her breath.

"Awe, come on, you're really going to be mad at me?" he asked her with pouted eyes.

She let out an exasperated sigh. "No. It's my own fault. I shouldn't let you talk me into such frivolous things."

"Well... I had a wonderful lunch with you. Hanging out with you is my favorite thing to do and I'm not sorry at all if it got you in trouble in your world of structure and busyness." Genuineness coated his words as did firmness and her heart echoed them.

It was everything she could do to keep from showing him how deeply and adamantly she agreed with him but she refused to do so; reasoning instead that it was the responsible thing to do to resist his calls to chaos.

"Just... don't come by work anymore, ok? We can hang out here anytime and on the weekends too, but when I'm at work I need to focus on getting the job done." She attempted to say this with power and directness but the twinge of sadness in her heart somehow made it out of her mouth.

He looked back at her with compassion in his eyes. Tenderness and adoration wrapped around her as his stare became an almost tangible touch of affection. "Good night, tough girl, I'll see you tomorrow." And with that he walked back inside his apartment closing the sliding glass patio door behind him.

She tossed and turned all night, her mind racing. All night was a love affair with fear. Anxiety took her breath away, worry swept her off her feet, and uncertainty stirred up butterflies in her stomach. She, of course, blamed it all on the late night cup of coffee.

Clickity-clack, clickity-clack.

She was at work extra early the next morning; after all, she wasn't sleeping. She barely looked up from her desk all morning and hardly noticed as the office filled with other robotic workers. It wasn't until well after 1 o'clock that a familiar figure caught the corner of her eye.

What is HE doing here?!

She rushed over to him, the raggedy man.

"What are you doing here? I thought I told you not come by here!" she demanded in an angry whisper.

The words had all but left her mouth when a man she had never seen before came walking up. He was an older man with more salt than pepper hair, the paint covered hands of an artist, and bright green thin rimmed glasses. His eyes were warm and inviting and exuded wisdom.

"Are we getting coffee or what?" the man asked her friend playfully.

"Let's go!" he said, then turned to her and asked, "Wanna come?"

"What? No, I don't want to come! You're going to get me in trouble again!" she answered forcefully, crossing her arms defiantly.

The older man let out a disruptively loud burst of bellowing laughter. "You can never get in any real trouble when you're with me, silly girl! Come, join us for coffee."

Her eyes darted around the room and she was surprised to see that no one seemed to notice his loud outburst or even her empty station. Everyone just went about their business as usual.

Clickity-clack, clickity-clack.

She let out a long sigh, anxiously biting her lip. "Well... I guess one cup of coffee wouldn't hurt anything...."

"Score!" shouted the raggedy man, grabbing her in a headlock and pulling her in for a hug.

Together the three of them left the building and walked across the street to a small coffee shop. It was a quaint and homey place, the walls were covered in chalkboard paint and burlap and the atmosphere was drenched in peace. The smells of brewing coffee and freshly baked muffins instantly put her at ease; this was her paradise.

"How have I never been here before?" she mumbled to herself under her breath.

"Probably because you've been too busy," said the old man.

She was silent. He was right.

They each ordered their favorite coffee and sat down at a table near the window.

"So…" the old man started looking straight at her, "How are you? My son has told me a lot about you; He's very fond of you."

She was surprised to learn that the man was his father, but she smiled at the raggedy man. She was fond of him too. "Um… well, I'm good. I'm doing really well at work and moving up. Hopefully I'll win that employee of the month award soon!" The words sounded excited but brightness was missing from her eyes as she answered him.

"Hmmm." He took another sip of his coffee, and then looked up at her with true concern in his eyes. "But how are you?"

She was somewhat confused, hadn't she just answered that question? "I'm fine," she answered again, "just trucking along, working hard, and hoping for that award!"

The two men exchanged concerned looks. "I see what you mean, she's a stubborn one isn't she?" The old man said to her friend.

"You have no idea," he answered chuckling.

"Um, you guys know I'm sitting right here right?" she said somewhat miffed.

"Let me ask you something," began the man, "Have you ever actually seen anyone win that award that you're working so hard to gain?"

She thought for a moment and then shook her head. "But I mean, everyone talks about it and about all those amazing workers that have left The Company who probably won it!"

The man gave a small but sad laugh and shook his head. "It's amazing, isn't it? How easily one can be convinced of something, simply because it makes sense, and never question or go searching for the truth before giving up their whole life to pursue that something. That something that other people have said is important."

Another small sigh and another sip of coffee. "Do you know who I am?" he asked her.

She shrugged her shoulders and cocked her head towards the man sitting next to her, "His dad?"

He smiled at her. "Yes, I am that, but I am also the owner of The Company."

Her mouth dropped open in shock. He looked nothing like what she imagined the owner of The Company would look. No tailored suit or hundred dollar haircut, but messy and relaxed.

"It's far from what I wished for it to be when I first started it," he continued, "What was once a place for freedom, laughter, and life, is now a place of deadlines and quotas and expectation."

He held out his paint covered hands for her to see.

"I'm an artist, a creator, and where would art be without the freedom to express and explore and innovate? How can such things be accomplished with pressure and judgment?"

She saw sadness in his eyes. Not the kind of sadness she would expect of him, not sadness of disappointment or regret, but the kind of sadness that occurs when you watch someone you care about hurt.

"But... don't you want your employees to perform well?" she asked, still a bit confused by it all.

"I much rather have an office full of collaborating artists than of diligent employees," he answered her, with a sense of pleading in his voice.

Her heart leapt in her chest and she tried her best to hide her excitement. She had dreamt of the freedom to create, the space to express, and her passion burned deep in her soul, bubbling up like lava at the sound of possibility.

"So, what about the Employee of the Month award?" she asked, beginning to doubt its existence for the first time.

This time her raggedy friend answered, "Oh yeah that would be me, I have that award!" Reaching down deep into his pocket he pulled out a large gold coin and a wad of pocket lint. Engraved on it were the words, "Employee of the Month."

She was shocked. "What? Do you ever even go to work? I thought you just rode around on your motorcycle making trouble." She gave him a snarky grin.

He laughed heartily and replied with a smile, "I've already done all the work. I've checked all the spreadsheets, paid all the bills, and I've even done all the marketing and planning for the life of The Company. So now all that's really left to do is ride around on my motorcycle and make trouble." He gave her a wink. "It seems that most would rather continue doing the work they think is important rather than freely innovate and create knowing it has already been completed."

She hung her head. She understood the struggle. For so long she had spent her life in anarchy pursuing what she thought was freedom but what turned out to really be bondage. To relinquish her own control and be swept into what looked, to her, so much like chaos seemed wrong. Life of control and order seemed like a better alternative. It seemed so right and yet the numbness, the emptiness, still haunted her. Still, the ache in her heart for something more real sometimes seemed too much to bear and she yearned desperately for something, anything that would make her feel alive again.

Now she sat here listening to these two men, and she was offered the very thing she truly craved... freedom. Freedom to create instead of destroy. Freedom to engage instead of overpower. Freedom to trust instead of fear. Freedom to be passionate instead of timid, confident instead of suppressed, and relatable instead of judgmental. Freedom to live, to really live, and resurrect the dead places inside her own heart. How could she resist such an offer?

She looked up at them, the fire of determination aflame in her eyes, "I'm in!"

"Well it's about freaking time!" exclaimed the raggedy man wrapping her up in the tightest hug that she had ever received.

The old man smiled brightly. "Let's create something."

From that moment on she lived life freely, traveling the world with her raggedy friend, and creating beauty everywhere she went-- a life in screaming color. She wore ripped jeans, a paint stained t-shirt, and true joy. Together they rode around on the back of a motorcycle and started trouble, leaving the sights and sounds of her former life in the dust it kicked up.

Clickity-clack, clickity-clack.

BELATOR THE TATTOOED MOUNTAIN TROLL

A parable of behavior and identity

"There is a difference between chasing grace for what it gives and chasing it for Who grace is ... It is Jesus, not a message, that makes us who we are."

-Paul White

"I am learning more and more that grace frees you to see the truth about yourself with hope and not despair"

-Tullian Tchividjian

There once was a quaint town called Fames. It was a nice little town surrounded by grassy knolls that smelled of fresh flowers in the spring time. On the far edge of town ran a sparkling brook that brought cool, fresh water to its inhabitants. The sounds of water gently licking the smooth river stones could be heard from every corner of the town. Straddling the brook was a tall twisted tree. Its thick branches tangled in one another and from them hung large succulent fruit of all kinds. It is rumored that the fruit changed to fit the needs of the one who picked from it.

The town was filled with all manner of strange creatures. There were 5 foot tall centipedes who found going shoe shopping to be a hassle. There where small hippos no larger than the length of a ball point pen who lived in tiny houses made of the centipedes' old shoe boxes. There were lion headed men who wore nice suits and bought lots of hair gel and there were peacocks who wore oversized hats and gaudy jewelry to hide their unpruned feathers. Every creature, no matter what shape or size, was always well dressed and appeared happy. Nothing in their homes was ever out of place, each and every one as tidy as the one beside it.

Every day in Fames was exactly like the one preceding it. All the townspeople awoke at exactly 7am to eat breakfast with their families. For the children, school started promptly at 8am at which time the adults filled their roles in the town. Everyone was always precisely where they were supposed to be, no one was ever late, and no one was ever missing. They finished their day with dinner at exactly 7pm and all heads hit pillows at 11pm on the dot. Everyone in the town had their place, everyone had their duties, everyone was comfortable, and no one asked questions.

On the far outskirts of the town was a tall cliff that overlooked the town and in this cliff was a hollowed out cave wherein lived a small mountain troll named Belator. Belator was the most beautiful of mountain trolls (if a mountain troll can be beautiful). Every day she sat with her legs dangling off the cliff outside her cave, watching the sunrise peek over the distant hills, and stared down on the city. It looked quite beautiful from her perch. She could smell the wafting aroma of the fresh flowers and hear the echoes of the brook bounce off the walls of her cave. She swore she could even taste the sweet fruit from the twisted tree which for her was always nectarines.

Belator was different than the other inhabitants of Fames. Her home was a dark and musty cave that was, if you asked her, wonderfully grungy. Along the walls grew thin vines on which hung a lovely little plant that was something like a vanilla bean, its smell seeped into her skin. She was very fond of these beans, often times clipping one to drop in her coffee as it brewed. Her clothes were disheveled and worn from use. They had frayed edges and loosely hanging buttons, none of which bothered her much.

She didn't wake up in sync with the others; in fact, she was often out of bed before the sun came up, stoking the fire to cook her breakfast and warm her coffee. She did this so that at precisely 7am she could watch as the tiny dots in the distance scurried across the town like ants, off once again to keep to their schedules.

Belator didn't have a schedule, not like the rest of them anyway, instead she spent the daylight hours collecting odd stones from the mountain and branches from the rainbow eucalyptus trees that grew at the bottom her cliff. These she used to sculpt into elegant pieces of art which served no purpose at all really except that she found them to be beautiful.

Her only companion on the mountain was Amar. Amar was a cute little creature, half wooly mammoth and half piglet. He was a small thing, no bigger than a fist, covered in silver fur with long curved red tusks, and a short little pig snout. Belator found Amar one day while looking for stones on an especially dangerous slope of the mountain in the middle of the most awful thunderstorm of the year. He was curled up, alone, and frightened under a large rock. He was desperately trying to stay dry, left behind by his herd because he was too small to keep up with them. Belator scooped him into her arms, tucked him under her cloak, and took him home; giving him food and making up a warm bed for him by the fire. They had been inseparable ever since.

This morning she sat in her usual spot, the crisp morning air tickling her bare feet as they swung back and forth over the cliff's edge. She watched the morning's activity with a twinge of dread stinging in the pit of her stomach. She glanced over her shoulder to the scarce pile of supplies that needed replenishing. She had known for a while now that it was time once again to voyage into town and restock her stores, but she had been putting it off as long as she could. She hated going into town. She would much rather admire it from afar.

Long ago, before there were schedules, before there were tidy houses, before there were roles, and before everyone was always precisely where they were supposed to be, Belator had lived in the town of Fames. She had the smallest cottage nearest the grassy knoll. You could tell which was hers by the large muddy footprints that marked the entryway. Things were different then. People were different then. Change, progression, and the invention of the clock all pushed Fames into the era of the deadline, and for creatures like Belator it meant they no longer fit in.

She sighed and begrudgingly got to her feet.

"Well, we might as well get this over with," she said grumpily to Amar. Amar snorted in protest.

"We do have to eat after all, you know."

Belator began cutting some beans from the vines around the cave. The people of Fames used her beans as fertilizer to grow shrubbery and various other plants that made the town look well put together. She would be able to trade them for food and other supplies once she arrived. Amar hooked a bag on his tusks and dragged it over to be filled. In no time at all the bag had been filled to the brim and Belator zipped it closed, tossing it into a large cart parked by the entrance. She also added a few empty jars to fill with honey and sweet milk, an empty bag to fill with fruit from the twisted tree, and one of her favorite pieces of art.

She shook the dust off her best outfit and slipped it on. She shook her head as she looked down at the pants held together by unmatched patches and poorly stitched thread. *This will just have to do,* she thought to herself.

"Come on then," she said to Amar as she picked him up and let him climb into the pocket of her jacket. He looked up at her with pleading eyes.

"Don't look at me like that. You know I don't like it any more than you do but it has to be done. Besides, it's not all bad. We can even stop by the twisted tree before we leave and maybe pick some flowers on our way home for the table?"

Amar's eyes brightened and he gave a slight nod in agreement.

Belator began her trek down the mountain, pushing her cart ahead of her. The mountain road was a rough and windy road with sharp drop offs in some spots, but Belator knew the mountain like the back of her hand and was down it and across the grassy knoll in no time, soon nearing the edge of town.

The town was alive with the hustle and bustle of activity. Jingles of shop bells, feet scurrying across sidewalks, and voices engaging in conversations were the sounds of the city. However, it seemed as if the clunking of Belator's cart loudly overpowered all the other noises. People shot sideways glances her way, and others moved to the opposite side of the street to avoid her. The peacocks snickered at her as she passed and the faint sounds of their conversation made their way to Belator's ears. "Will you just look at that outfit, I mean really, she could at least *try* to look a little more put together."

Belator was familiar with those whispers.

She quickly and silently made her way to Rix General Store. Mr. Rix was a descendant of the dinosaurs. He was a tall slender man who looked much like a Velociraptor but with smooth skin and a long tail (which often came in handy when restocking shelves). He had a thick well-groomed mustache and a deep crackly voice that made Belator uneasy. He was helping a well-dressed female centaur when Belator lumbered in. He looked disapprovingly her way.

"It's that time again, is it?" he asked annoyed.

"Yes, sir. I brought as many beans as would fit in my bag this time," she answered trying to force a smile.

"We will deal with it in a minute!" he shot back.

The centaur curled her lip and leaned over the counter whispering to Mr. Rix, "You'd think she'd at least make sure she doesn't smell like fertilizer when coming in to town; it's absolutely repulsive!"

Amar growled angrily.

"I'm sure they didn't mean for me to hear," she said softly to him.

The centaur gave her a wide berth as she exited quickly, holding her nose in order to get her point across. Amar rolled his eyes, and Belator tried to inconspicuously sniff her clothes. *Is it really that bad?* She wondered? Her thoughts were derailed by Mr. Rix's bellowing.

"Aye! I don't have all day!"

She pulled the bag up onto the counter and opened it to reveal the contents. The sweet vanilla smell filled the air.

"Oh, come on, close it up! I don't want that horrid smell driving my customers away! It looks like plenty, go ahead and take what you want," Mr. Rix said irritated.

Belator didn't move.

"Didn't you hear me, troll, or are you deaf too? I said go ahead!"

"Well... I brought this too..." she began and she pulled out the sculpture, "and I was just wondering if maybe you'd like to have it? It's quite beautiful as you can see."

"What does it do?" he asked expectantly.

"Well, it doesn't *do* anything, it just is," she answered.

Mr. Rix inspected the item carefully. It seemed like hours to Belator before he finally gave his answer. "Why would I want something that doesn't do anything when I have a fancy gear operated clock made by the finest clock maker in town that is both beautiful and tells me what time it is?" He motioned to the large wooden clock hanging above the counter as he shook his head. "Stick to fertilizer; that's what you're good for. Now go on, get your supplies and be on your way, I'll have more customers soon."

Belator, discouraged, placed the sculpture carefully back in her cart and began filling it with the supplies she needed from the store. Amar snuggled up against her hoping to make her feel a little better.

"Oh well," she said, "Maybe next time. "

When her cart was full and Mr. Rix had dramatically emptied out the fertilizer bag while wearing a gas mask and handing it back to her using only two fingers, she left the store and headed across town to the twisted tree. The twisted tree was her favorite part of coming to the city. Few people came to visit it anymore now that their lives were filled with responsibility and deadlines, but it was once the focal point of the town. Everyone would come to pick fruit from its branches, anxious to see what their special fruit would be. Once, when the town had all but withered away and the brook had dried up, the twisted tree still stood strong, bearing fruit of all kinds. The starving people of Fames flocked to its branches picking all that they could hold. Just as you would begin to think that the fruit would run out, like magic, they grew back as fast as they were picked. Everyone had all but forgotten that story. Except for Belator, that is.

She told Amar the story for the 100th time as they ate their fruit together—nectarines for her and limes for him. She pulled off her shoes and let the cool water of the brook gently caress her calloused feet.

"That was a long time ago," she told Amar, "People were different then… kinder."

A single tear streaked down her dusty cheek.

"I don't understand what's so awful about me. Am I really that disgusting of a creature?" she asked, her voice trembled a little as she struggled to hold back tears. Amar curled into her lap trying to comfort her.

"Who told you that you were disgusting?" asked a strange voice that seemed to be coming from the tree.

"Uh… I… I'm not sure I feel comfortable talking to an inanimate object," she said matter-of-factly.

The branches shook and she heard an amused laugh.
"I'm not a big fan of it laughing at me either," she said sternly.

The branches shook again and from among them emerged a man. Belator had never seen any creature like this man before. He was tall and muscular with disheveled brown hair. A short, scruffy beard covered his face behind which was a smile that drew you into it. His eyes were kind and his forehead wrinkled with expressiveness. He wore ripped jeans, battered black and white shoes that looked not unlike Belator's, and a mud stained white tank top. From what she could tell, every bit of skin on his body was beautifully adorned in what looked like drawn on words. She read a few-- *loved, accepted, perfect, beauti...*

"I'm not a tree," he said jokingly, "Does that mean you'll answer my question?"

She looked at him puzzled, "Who are you?"

"I'm Finn," he answered, "I take care of the tree. Now, Belator, who told you that you're disgusting?"

Belator looked at him aghast. "How... how do you know my name? Nobody knows my name."

"I've been around a very long time. In fact, I remember when you were born and when you left the city to live in the mountain and I watch you come here every month and tell the story of the tree to your adorable little friend there." His words were soft and gentle and for some reason that she couldn't explain, put her at ease.

"Oh," she said almost inaudibly as she was flooded with memories. "I guess that makes more sense than you being a tree." She gave him a snarky half smile.

"It does make a better story the other way around though!" He winked at her.

She smiled at him and shook her head.

"Belator. Who told you that you are disgusting?"

Her smiled faded, "Everyone," she answered ashamed.

"Not me," he said with a kindness she had not seen in many years. Amar grunted in agreement.

"You… you don't think I'm disgusting?" She asked in shock. "Of course not! I find you to be delightful, actually," he said raising his eyebrows and giving her a reassuring smile. "And what is that scent? Is that vanilla I smell? It's lovely!"

Her eyes brightened, "It's my beans. They grow on the vines that creep across the walls of my cave. Most people can't stand the smell…"

He took a seat next to her by the brook and caught her staring at his arms.

"Do you know what they are?" he asked her.

"No. I think they are beautiful whatever they are," she answered.

"They are called tattoos. My father gave them to me. I'm very fond of them!" He explained. "They help me take care of the tree and the people of Fames. They make me strong and confident and they protect me from people who call me disgusting."

"People call you disgusting?" she quizzed, awestruck. (She didn't think he was disgusting at all).

"Oh yes, but they are wrong. See?" He pointed to a word on his arm—*Perfect.*

"I wish I had some of those," she said sadly. Amar barked as if to say, "Me too!"

"Would you like some?" he asked her.

She looked up at him excitedly, "Oh yes, very much!"

"I can give you some if you'd like?" he offered.

"That would be wonderful! I don't have much but I can give you some of my beans, they are delicious in coffee!" She was joyful, as she jumped to her feet ready to hurry back to the cave to get them.

"I require no payment from you," he said softly. "All I ask, is that you come here to the tree every day so that I can give them to you."

"You mean... I have to come to town... *every* single day?" She said hesitantly.

"Yes, and I know that it will be a difficult journey, but I promise every day I will be here waiting to give you a new tattoo," he reassured her.

"Alright. I'll do it." She held her head high, resolute in her decision. She caught a glimpse of the pink and purple sunset stained sky. "Oh! I better be going before it gets dark!" She exclaimed.

"Have a safe trip home, I will be waiting here for you tomorrow." He waved goodbye as she joyfully pushed her cart back towards the mountain. As the day shut its eyes, she pulled her cart into the cave, quickly changed out of her fancy "going to town" outfit, and unloaded her supplies. Her mind raced with wonder at the day's events.

That night she was much too excited to sleep. She tossed and turned as she thought of how beautiful her arms would look covered in her new tattoos. Finally, her eye lids became too heavy and she drifted off into a sweet slumber.

She awoke the next morning even earlier than usual, hurriedly preparing breakfast and getting ready for her trip. She hardly noticed the first rays of sunlight creeping over the horizon as she nudged a sleeping Amar.
"Come on, wake up! We have to go to the tree; Finn will be waiting!" She shouted

Amar winced, snorted defiantly, and turned over to go back to sleep.

"Fine. Have it your way. I'll just go without you then!" She said bluntly. And with that she darted out the entrance to her cave, unaware that she was not very well dressed for a trip into town.

She had never gone to town without her cart before and the walk seemed much more enjoyable without it clunking in front of her. *I wonder if Finn will really be waiting for me,* she thought to herself as she walked through the flower covered knoll. *I wonder what tattoo he will give me first? I wonder how you get tattoos anyway? Maybe he has a special magic pen or somethi..* BAM! Her thoughts were interrupted as she crashed into a large monocle wearing turtle. She had been so distracted thinking about getting to the tree that she had not even noticed that she had already arrived in town.

"Well, I never! Is it acceptable to just run over whomever you desire up on your mountain? And if I am going to be run over I'd at least like it to be by someone well dressed, would you just look at your clothes!" The turtle exclaimed indignantly as he picked himself off the ground, meticulously dusting off the dirt. "Quite ugly indeed."

Belator looked down at her clothes in shame, "I... must have forgotten." She stammered.

"Hmph. I suggest you tend to that immediately." He stuck his nose in the air and hurried off to his respectable life with better dressed people.

She sprinted the rest of the way to the twisted tree, the wind blowing silent tears across her face as she ran. When she finally made it to the brook she slumped next to the tree and wiped a large glob of snot from her nose with her sleeve. Finn hung upside down and poked his head out from the branches of the tree startling her.

"Why are you crying?" he asked compassionately.

"Because I am ugly," she answered, sniffling.

"Who told you that you were ugly?" He questioned her as he jumped down from the tree and sat beside her.

"A very well dressed turtle. He had nice clothes and a monocle, he must know what beautiful looks like," said Belator.

"Hmm." He grunted, unconvinced. "Let me ask you, does he know you? Does he know that you are kind and caring to even the smallest of creatures? Does he know that you are brave and respectful even when it is hard?"

"Well, no, in fact, he doesn't know me at all." She looked up and wiped the last of her tears away with her snot stained sleeve.

"Then what does it matter what he calls you?"

This was an odd question, one that Belator had never thought to consider before. As he asked her this, he reached down, pulled up her snotty sleeve, and brushed the inside of her forearm with his thumb. Belator looked down to see a fantastic sight. Right before her eyes, by what *must* have been some kind of magic, appeared the gorgeous swoops and curves of a word. She read it to herself—*beautiful.* She giggled in delight and looked up to see Finn smiling sweetly at her. He held out his arm to show her his matching tattoo in the same place.

"Look." He motioned to his arm, "We match!"
At that she gave him a hug that was more like a tackle. "Thank you so much! It's wonderful!"

Smiling brightly, he attempted to catch his breath from her hug tackle. "Now, next time someone tells you that you are ugly, show them you are beautiful," he said nodding towards her arm.

She nodded at him in agreement. They spent the rest of the afternoon talking and laughing together. Finn began to teach her how to take care of the twisted tree, how to prune its branches and pull up the weeds around its roots. Belator had the best day in a long time and was sad to say goodbye when the time came to head back to the mountain.

"See you tomorrow!" He yelled at her as she walked into the distance.

She couldn't wait.

That night after dinner she walked down to the base of mountain into the forest of rainbow eucalyptus trees. Between two especially stout trees hung a weather worn hammock. There she lay with Amar on her chest, the sweet minty smell of the trees filling the air. She pulled her arm up and stared at the tattoo.

"It was strange..." she explained to Amar "...he touched my arm and it was like the tattoo raised up from under my skin. Like... like it had been just hiding beneath the surface the whole time."

Amar looked at it, cocked his head, then looked at her and nodded approvingly.

"Beautiful. Because I am beautiful," she said trying to convince herself more than him.

They fell asleep there under the stars, the cool night air rocking the hammock back and forth rhythmically. Belator was awakened the next morning by Amar licking her face; he didn't want to miss the trip this time. "Gross!" She said pushing him away "I'm up, I'm up!"

She rolled out of the hammock, Amar crawled on to her shoulder, and they took off towards the town. As they entered Fames, a loud demanding grumble came from the pit of Belator's stomach. *I completely forgot about breakfast!* She thought. "What do you think?" She asked Amar, pointing towards the diner at the end of the street. "Breakfast?" Amar nodded hungrily, a small gurgle coming from his stomach.

There weren't many people in the diner, but those who were seemed horrified that she had entered. She sat at the farthest table in the corner, trying to stay out of the way. A small, duck-billed, green hedgehog came and took her order for pancakes and sweet milk. While she waited, Belator looked around the diner, feeling the air of uncomfortableness thicken. She saw a small group circled around a booth across from her. There sat a very attractive, sophisticated phoenix. She wore long ruby earrings and when her feathers caught the sun the orange and red sparkle made the whole diner look like it was on fire. She was surrounded by what looked to be her friends, at least ten of them, all laughing at her jokes and looking at her adoringly.

The phoenix kept looking over at Belator, at which point Belator decided to spend the remainder of her visit to the diner staring down at her table and pretending not to exist. After what seemed like an eternity, her pancakes arrived and she split them with Amar, drowning them in syrup and scarfing them down less than eloquently.

"AHEM!" Belator looked up from her plate, syrup stickily dripping from her chin, to see the phoenix standing at her table with her posse.

"Just exactly what do you think that *you* are doing here?" The phoenix questioned snottily.

"Jus' eatin' breafask," Belator answered, mouth half full of her last bite of pancakes.

"Ew," said the phoenix with a curled lip. "No one wants a reject like you here; you are ruining the pleasant morning atmosphere of the place. Can't you just leave already?"

The rest of the diner clapped in agreement.

"Oh. I'm sorry," she said sorrowfully, wiping her mouth and picking up a sticky Amar. "We'll get out of your way." She left the diner with head hung, slowly making her way towards the twisted tree. Amar looked up at her and whimpered.

"It's ok. She was just telling the truth," she said dejected.

When they got to the brook, Belator washed the syrup off of Amar in the water and set him free to play in the grass along its banks. She picked up a smooth stone and skipped it across the water.

"Hello again!" Said a familiar voice behind her.

"Hello..." she said halfheartedly.

"You seem sad this morning; what's the matter?" Finn asked her.

"I'm a reject," Belator answered plainly.

"Who told you that you are a reject?" he asked with concern in his eyes.

"A beautiful phoenix. She had so many friends. She must know what being accepted looks like," she said with a tremor in her voice, refusing to let the tears shake loose this time.

"Beautiful Belator..." he began softly taking her arm and raising it to show her the tattoo, "...Does she know you? Does she know that you are the most loyal friend anyone could have? Does she know that you care for Amar better than even his own family did? Does she know that your laugh can light up a room or that time spent with you is never wasted?"

Belator shook her head and gave him a half smile. He caressed her arm again next to her first tattoo and a new one slowly faded into view—*Treasured.* Belator ran her fingers over it checking to make sure it wouldn't come off.

"Next time someone calls you a reject, show them that you are treasured." He held up his arm next to hers showing once again that they matched.

Her still syrup stained lips stretched wide into a smile and she called out, "Amar, come look at this!" The rest of the day they all spent together taking care of the tree and telling their favorite stories from the old times by the end of which Belator had forgotten all about the rude phoenix and her stuck up friends. As evening neared Amar and Belator headed for home, both giving Finn a hug and promising to return in the morning.

Every day for the next 364 days, Belator would travel into town, to the banks of the babbling brook at the base of the twisted tree. Every day, Finn would remind her that she was beautiful and treasured and loved and chosen and perfect. Soon, Belator had as many tattoos as Finn and was running out of places to put them. From the tops of her ears to the tip of her big toe were written beautiful words in elegant letters that she couldn't imagine living without. Every day for 364 days, the people of Fames were much too busy with places to go and things to do to notice that the once clear skinned Belator was now covered in tattoos. Then, on the 365th day, something different happened.

Belator walked confidently into town. This year had changed her. She no longer hung her head in shame as the people on the street gawked at her. She no longer worried if her smell made people uncomfortable or if her clunking cart was annoying. She just was and she was happy. Finn had given her a spotless (at the time) white tank top that matched his. It now had sweat stains, dirt smudges, and sap from working on the tree. Nevertheless, she wore it proudly.

She noticed as she headed out towards the brook that there was a large gathering in the center of the town. It looked like some kind of town wide celebration and she walked over to investigate it. There were carts full of food and colored toys lining the outside of the square, people wore clothes that seemed even more fancy than usual, and brightly colored streamers hung from rooftops. Belator snatched a powdered donut from a cart as she walked down the street. She thought back to long ago when she lived in Fames. *Today must be the 100 year anniversary of the clock,* she thought to herself. Sure enough as she walked down the extravagantly decorated streets she saw the time keeping hands of clocks drawn on every banner. She heard a loud voice coming from a speaker in the center of the town square. "Gather 'round, gather 'round!"

The mayor of Fames was a large, potbellied orangutan. His bright orange fur was trimmed and combed down into a high society side part. He wore a spotless three piece suit with gold banana shaped cufflinks and black and white wing-tipped shoes. Perched on his abnormally large nose sat a pair of diamond encrusted bifocals that sparkled in the sunlight. He cleared his throat and started again, "Gather 'round one and all and welcome to the centennial celebration of our most prized invention!"

Belator snorted at the silliness of it all which caused her to inhale an unfortunate amount of powdered sugar from atop her donut. She subsequently let out a large and earth shaking sneeze. *ACHOO!*

The entire town turned to look at her. She gulped.

"What are *YOU* doing here?!" Demanded the mayor.

"I was just passing through," Belator started, "and it looked like it would be fun to stop by."

The mayor sneered in disapproval. "No one wants an ugly reject like you messing up this perfectly nice celebration. Go run along now and play in the mud or whatever it is that trolls do. You aren't needed here."

Belator turned to walk away then sharply turned back, pushing back the beginnings of tears, and speaking forcefully. "I am NOT ugly. I am beautiful!" She said sternly, proudly lifting her arm to show everyone her tattoo. "See. It says so right here."

The entire town stared dumfounded, finally noticing the tattoo covered arms of the troll.

She continued... "And here, see, I am NOT a reject. I am treasured. And I am chosen and perfect and loved and smart and..." she listed off each and every name that she could see, declaring them with pride in her voice.

A raccoon faced man next to her ran his fingers down her arm admiringly. "Where did you get such beautiful markings?" He asked, astounded that they didn't rub off with his touch.

"My friend, Finn, gave them to me," she answered. "He lives down by the brook across town and takes care of the twisted tree. I help him take care of the tree now too!"

"Rubbish," grumbled the mayor, "complete rubbish."

"If you want some you can come visit him too. I'm sure he wouldn't mind!" She continued, unaffected by the mayor's disdain.

"Um... maybe later." Said the raccoon, frightened by the disapproving looks of those standing near him.

Belator shrugged, "Very well then, I'll leave you all to your boring clock party." And with that she skipped off across town to find Finn sitting against the trunk of the twisted tree. He motioned for her to come sit down beside him.

Plopping down she asked, "Not working on the tree today?"

"No, today I was just waiting for you. I have something I want to talk to you about," he answered.

"Ok!" she said excitedly wondering what it was.

"Do you remember your very fist tattoo?" he asked.

She smiled brightly and nodded vigorously.

"Do you remember how happy you felt and how much it changed you?"

"It was the most wonderful thing I have ever experienced!" she answered joyfully.

Smiling sweetly he continued, "Well now you are out of room for tattoos and you are quite different than when you first started coming to see me; don't you think?"

She nodded again.

"Now it's time that I give you something else that my father gave me."

"What's that?" she questioned eagerly.

"A purpose," he said.

Belator looked at him quizzically.

"My purpose is to help people like you, Beautiful Belator. People who are truly magnificent but are unable to see it just yet. People who need friendship and love and kindness. My purpose it to help people see the tattoos that are hidden under the surface," Finn explained.

"And... what is my purpose?" Belator asked somewhat worried that she wouldn't know how to achieve it.

Finn put a reassuring hand on her shoulder. "Invite people to the tree."

"I tried that already," she explained. "Nobody wanted to come." A deflated look crossed her face.

"It's not your purpose to make them come," Finn said supportively. "It's your purpose to invite them. Invite them because you want them to experience what you've experienced here. Invite them because everyone should get to see their tattoos. It's a really great purpose and its one I know you will do splendidly!"

She smiled confidently up at him. "Alright then, I'll do it!"

And she did.

From that day forward, Beautiful Belator the tattooed mountain troll came to Fames proclaiming the wonderful things that could be found on the banks of the brook under the shade of the twisted tree. At first people laughed at her, but soon some followed her to the tree. Finn welcomed them and helped them each see the beautiful tattoos inked just below the surface of their skin. Amar and Belator were joined on their mountain by many other tattooed creatures including a once popular phoenix and an uptight monocle wearing turtle. Every day they would go, led by Belator, to the people of Fames, declaring the wonders found at the tree.

Not everyone followed them, some even thought that they had lost their minds, but those who did follow were drastically changed by what they found under their skin. They no longer kept tidy houses. They no longer rushed to be places on time. They no longer looked put together or acted prim and proper. They just were and they were happy.

Years passed, the hands on the prized clocks of Fames ticked away effortlessly, each stroke pushing the observers towards one deadline or another. Soon as many as watched them forsook them for the timeless tranquility they found at the twisted tree. What had started for Belator as a dreaded trip into the town that rejected her had become a life of love like she had never dreamed.

She looked around at all those who sat peacefully in the soft grass by the water's edge; sharing fruit and smiles. People who had once rushed by one another, who had treated one another badly, and even a once frightened raccoon faced man too afraid to take the first steps towards freedom, all sat there enjoying their time together. Time when watched seemed dreadfully oppressive, but now was more precious and powerful than ever. She smiled contentedly to herself and Finn walked her way tossing a nectarine from behind his back into her hand.

"It's beautiful isn't it?" He asked her, looking around.

"It is," she answered. "It is very beautiful."

"One day it will all be like this," he started.

"You mean the whole city of Fames?" She wondered.

"Yes," he answered, "And other cities like it. One day everyone will get to see their tattoos and enjoy life without schedules and eat fruit with the ones they love."

"That will be beautiful, won't it?" Belator asked, smiling at him.

"Yes. It will be very beautiful." He laughed pulling her with one arm into a hug. "Just like you," he added looking down at her very first tattoo.

Belator smiled up at him, "Just like me."

THE OCEAN, THE STORM, AND THE MERMAN

A parable of wreckage and rebirth

"If grace is an ocean then we are all sinking."

-The David Crowder Band

"When we seek to be free by our own will we live in bondage to our own abilities."

-Jenna Lang

Her tangled mess of red hair was wild and unruly. The fire in her eyes mimicked it and her skin smelled of cheap sunscreen and sea salt. She wasn't the smartest or the strongest or the best at anything but she was mediocre at enough things to make hubris her vice. No one thought much of her, well, except for her of course.

She was independent to a fault, refusing to ask for help even in her most dismal times. If anger was a person, she was it—red hair, fiery eyes, explosive soul. The only thing that seemed to douse the flames inside her was the ocean.

She would walk the beaches at night, writing, thinking, and wishing she was different. She wished she were different because though she had pride to spare she also had insecurity enough to keep her from flying too high. She was a paradox of self-righteousness and self-loathing which caused her to revile both criticism and compliments. She was angst but here, on the beach, there was peace.

The beach's cool waters soaked the embers in her and left the smokes of rest wafting from her. Here in the silence is where she was most herself. If only she could allow herself to stay here. No, her unwavering sense of responsibility would not allow her to do so, after all, there was no way the world could get along without her. And so she would leave her life along the beach to return to her world of importance where she smugly faced adversity and claimed significance while inwardly struggling to find either. She haughtily feigned humility thinking both too highly and not enough of herself.

She had always been this way, even as a young child. With tussled hair and poor hygiene she would confidently correct those around her in an anxious attempt to grasp at significance. She always was a mystery even, and maybe more so, to herself. This was her identity until one dark and stormy night along the coastline when her life was changed forever.

Though the storm brought heavy rain and loud thunder, she did not forsake her walk along the beach that night. She didn't mind the storm; in fact, some part of her found solace in it. The way the skies thrashed and screamed under the weight of their purpose reminded her that even the clouds were unhappy sometimes and were eager to grumble along with her. That night she felt much like a raging sea trapped inside a rain drop and was comforted by the more tangible deluge of water that showered down upon her.

She was so caught up in the beauty of the storm that she had forgotten the danger of it, and before she knew it the tide had risen and swept her out to sea. She swam desperately for the shore, scooping water frantically behind her as she fought the strong current that pulled her farther and farther out into the deep waters that she loved so much. The tempestuous waters won with ease and despite using every bit of strength and power she had within her she was overcome by them. The waves were now walls of water, and the ferocious winds of the storm drove them towards her. The waves came crashing down upon her and she was buried beneath their foamy fingers. All she could see around her was blue, her chest ached for air. She flailed for the surface but could not reach it. The salt stung her eyes but still she willed them open staring into the blue... and then black.

The next thing she saw when she opened her eyes was bright lights hanging from a beautiful chandelier fashioned from coral and sea shells. Death must have found her for surely this was heaven, she thought. As her eyes adjusted she came to a startling realization—she was still underwater! But... she could breathe, how was this possible? She spun around in the water weightlessly, in awe of her surroundings. The more she looked around the more she began to believe that she was in a large castle made of coral. The walls were brightly colored and porous. The doors and handles were all gaudily adorned with gold fixtures. She pulled back the seaweed curtain nearest the bed she had been lying on to see the shocking and overwhelming world of ocean life swirling around her. Fish of all kinds and colors darted quickly back and forth, large sea turtles coasted casually, crabs scurried along the ocean floor, and... wait... what was that she saw? Was that a mermaid?! Certainly this must be the afterlife she decided undoubtedly.

She stood there awkwardly, mouth agape, as a merman came swimming through the window into her room. She stared at him awestruck. From the waist up he was muscular but not defined. He had muscles that were more likely to come from hard labor than from weight training. His knuckles and shoulders were scarred from, what she imagined, was some heroic feat. He had a long, brightly colored, finned tail that was made up of different shades of red and orange (much like her hair). She noticed that his tail was missing a few scales, tattered from a life under the sea she supposed.

He never said an audible word to her, but much like the ocean his silence spoke volumes to her spirit and her soul was soothed by him. He flashed her a smile and his dark brown eyes swept her away. He looked sweetly at her and grabbed her by the hand, beckoning her to adventure the unfamiliar waters beyond the coral castle. She did not resist his pull, excited to discover this new and exciting world.

Days went by, months, years, she did not know really for she was caught up in the timeless swirl of him. They explored far and wide the depths of this world. Just when she thought they had seen it all he would reveal to her a new place, a previously unknown corner, and she would be mesmerized by it. Soon she became comfortable in her new world. The colors didn't seem as shockingly bright as they once did, the water became as common as air, and she determined that she no longer needed to adventure with him but could do some discovery on her own. Apparently, an independent will is not as easily drowned as the body.

One night she sneaked out, paddling cumbersomely through the familiar waters. As comfortable as her new home was, legs are simply not efficient for aquatic travel. The farther she swam on her own, the harder it became for her to breathe. At first she thought it was just fatigue, but the further she went the tighter her chest clenched, until finally her last breath was accompanied by a large gulp of water. She choked and coughed and tried desperately to breathe again but it was futile. She was once again tossed by the ferocity of the sea and unable to regain control of herself. Just as she gave up fighting and allowed herself to float helplessly she felt two strong arms pull her into an embrace. As her head hit his chest she breathed deeply and her lungs were filled with life once again.

She looked up at him confused. She didn't understand what just happened. He explained to her that here in the ocean independence leads only to pain. The more you fight the current the more you become a victim to it. The beautiful ebb and flow of its waters could quickly turn into a drowning liquid grave for every ounce of effort you had left in you. She then began to understand that the ocean was both soothing and abrasive for she would have to learn to lean on his company to explore it further.

She never became as dependent as she should have, and there were many more nights of freelance swimming, but the more secure she became in his companionship the deeper and more beautiful were the waters they explored. Each new adventure in the briny depths revealed new and wondrous things not only about it, but also about her. She was shocked to discover the truth of herself; that she was not at hard and fiery as she seemed. In his company through these cerulean currents, she began to see that she was both incredibly significant and utterly unimportant. This may seem like a negative view I know, but it was incredibly freeing for she had lived so long in bondage to her own importance that finding worth apart from it brought a peace beyond description.

She still lives there, under the liquid sapphire blanket. Rebellious nights still leave her gasping for air until she is rescued once again by strong, scarred arms. More numerous than these are the days spent discovering the sparkling infinity of the waters and the smallest recesses of her own heart. She will never tire of being surprised by both.

SHE: AS TOLD BY HIM

A parable of true love

"In this is love: not that we have loved God, but that he loved us and sent his Son to be the atoning sacrifice for our sins."

-1 John 4:10

She is a mess of gorgeous chaos. A beautiful paradox of calm and calamity, she swings from moment to moment between the addiction to order and the urge for anarchy. Some would see these as negative qualities, but I don't. From the moment I saw her I loved her. I have persisted to love her with a love that she still cannot comprehend for I see depths within her that even oceans cannot fathom. I know her better even than she knows herself, which she has said can be quite annoying at times.

I know pieces of her heart that she has hidden in the dark corners of her being, too afraid to look upon them for fear that they may be too unruly for even me to tame. Silly girl, as if she could hide anything from me. She is afraid of the dark but I go spelunking through the caverns of her soul and see beauty where the light bounces off the walls. One day she will see it and I will spend eternity beckoning her to adventure inside herself with me.

What is she like you ask? She is still water and she is a hurricane. Her messy hair is a visible attribute of her stubborn spirit but she still lets me run my fingers through it. The dark chocolate brown of her eyes flicker between confidence and insecurity but remain a temptation towards freedom to those who catch a glimpse of them. She says she wants to be a writer but what she really wants is to be someone's muse. She wears what she calls shortcomings like armor, and her darkness like a little black dress. She is naïve to her perfection. She is splendor and I cannot help but be in awe of her.

Some mornings I catch her looking in the mirror, poking at the bulging curves and edges of her body, the crease in her brow revealing her distaste with what she sees. She rarely believes me when I tell her so, but she is a fiery heart and an untainted spirit. Still, she insists on being defined by her shell and I long for her to see her worth. She calls it madness that I dote on her so and I remind her that love makes a fool of reason.

In her lifetime she has faced monsters whose ugliness she still finds hard to speak of. Monsters which she found more often hiding under her bed than in the dangerous places she was warned to avoid. Even still, she lives a vibrant life for even as my heart was wrenched in sadness at the sight of her struggle I never once left her side in the mist of it. My love for her is so great I willingly bore the punishment the monsters should have received so that she would be spared the pain of injustice. She may never fully understand this act but knowing that did not stop me from doing it.

My girl. My resplendent woman. My most loved one. I could never love her less.

Someone came to me once, accusing her of unspeakable acts, her former lover I believe it was. He called her a whore claiming that she had one affair after another, getting into bed with anyone who might quench her need for satisfaction. He called me ignorant for loving her, said that after each affair she would crash devastatingly into the reality of her faithlessness and come running back to my arms desperate for my love.

He claimed that I trustingly embraced her and was confused as to how I could. His accusations enraged me, but not as you would think they would. See, it is he who is the ignorant one. How ridiculous of him to think such stories could ever dim her identity. What an incredulous plan, to come to *me* whispering the lies that only the faithless believe, to I who am always faithful. I guess he just hasn't figured out yet that our relationship is built upon my love for her and not the other way around. Our marriage remains pure and untainted as it always shall. I reminded her of this fact when, after his lies didn't work on me and he told them to her, she came questioning our union.

I need her head on my heart; she needs to hear it beat for her. And as she lays with me I will kiss every scar on her beautiful heart so that they become markings of a love that survives pain. We will be together and she will forget the rest. Together we will always be poetry in a world that is still learning the alphabet, our immortal stanzas ever enduring to bring art to a world oblivious of its purpose.

She is the moon and I the sun; I delight every day to die so that she might have life. No one knows her as I do, not even her. She is a mess of gorgeous chaos and I am pleased to be tangled up in her.

Final Thoughts

Much of this year was a hard one. I spent a lot of time in chaos and confusion as I felt layers of my own pride and self-righteousness stripped away and my eyes opened to the bigger and better reality of what Christ IN ME really means. It's been a beautifully messy journey in understanding what my true identity is and a humbling experience to realize that it's all apart from my own abilities.

Tullian Tchividjian once said in one of his sermons, "If you're afraid to let people see your badness what that reveals is that you have built your identity on the appearance of being good." I was not aware of how truly afraid I was of others seeing my badness, my ugliness, and the unrenewed pieces of my soul until I began putting onto paper all my places of faithlessness. As I began to unpack this heavy baggage I had carried for so long it felt much like I was simultaneously drowning from waves and dying of thirst.

I now lay before you exposed.   You know me or, at least, some of the more intimate parts of my struggle. I am every she and Christ is every he and I am still learning to believe that he and she are meant to be intimately intertwined in one another. Despite her independence, her addiction, her bondage, or even her ugliness as seen by others, she is and always will be his.

It's interesting to read these pieces now as one collection, and in doing so I am reminded of the great significance of the journey. It's quite beautiful to see the different personalities of God's grace and how each one is able to speak the different languages of my heart.

I'd be lying if I said that I've figured it all out. Just because I have put pen to paper and resolved it in ink in no way means that my soul ceases to struggle in understanding it all. I know very little of the vast grace of God-- only that it pursued me relentlessly in the midst of my unfixedness to make me new. Therefore, I reason, it can never be frightened away by the jagged edges of my humanity. Instead, it reminds me that I am not defined by them. Because of this truth I am determined to wear these jagged edges proudly as if they were badges of brokenness God has polished with His wholeness.

Often we're afraid of our own ugliness. So then it's easier for us to be enraged about the "big" issues in our world, to throw a fit over unisex bathrooms, to spew hatred over people's choices at the polls, and to mock legalistic pastors. It is much easier for us to face the monsters we see in the world than it is to face the ones under our bed.

And in neglecting to face the monsters under our beds, we effectively sabotage the great story of redemption. For it is only in the most desperate and most unmanageable of moments that we can truly see the ineffable glory of grace and its ability to conquer even the most ruthless of foes.

Maybe that's what Jesus meant when he said, "those who have been forgiven much love much." Maybe his words were not meant as qualifiers of the greatness of one's love but rather exposers of the depth of one's need.

Only when we are brave enough to come out from under the covers and meet the monsters we imagine to be formidable face to face are we able to see them whimpering and wailing under the rescuing fist of God's grace. It is inevitable that in these moments we will be brought to our knees once again in awe and wonder of a God who transcends our situation and yet is intimately aware of our pain.

We want to tame grace, to lasso it, and tie it down to the pew next to us. It bucks and jumps and lays to waste the structured box of a building we've placed it in like a bull in a china shop. Grace is not safe. It saves. There's a big difference between the two. It will hazardously force you to have to face the monsters under your bed but it will also rescue you from them. I wish we would allow ourselves to be brave enough to look under our beds. Then maybe, just maybe, in being honest about the monsters under our beds we might find that the ones in the world aren't as big as they seemed.

In so many ways this book has been an etching of my facing the monsters under my bed. This is my attempt to expose my own broken places with the eager hope that it encourages others to do the same. I desperately wish for each one of you, whoever you may be, you who finds yourself reading this book to be encouraged to look at your own places of brokenness with hope and not despair.

I vividly remember this moment I had with God in the midst of this journey. I was so frustrated with how things didn't seem to be working out the way I wanted them to and I watched as cracks began to form along the well-constructed emotional walls I had built. I was frantically running around trying to patch the holes and I heard this whisper in my spirit say to me, "Jess, why are you trying to preserve what I want to destroy?" It was from that moment that I began to believe that brokenness had less to do with punishment and more to do with healing.

So often we think of brokenness as the ending point. We see it as the negative result of something destructive happening to a thing which was once whole. What if it's actually the other way around? What if, in reality, we all begin broken and the true beauty of our new creation is built out of the rubble of our broken beginning. What if wholeness is the result of brokenness?

We all wish to believe that our original perfect state of wholeness is that of a ship. It sails freely and majestically on the water; and yet, some fierce and unrelenting storm rages and the ship ends up shipwrecked. How easy it is for us to relate to this, that at one time all was good and now it's not. We all vainly wish for our origin story to be birthed in the majesty of a calm sea. The truth is our origin is not in the ship but in the shipwreck. We all begin as tattered sails and rotted wood and it is only in our recognition of that fact that we can see the true beauty in the new creation the Artist has fashioned from the wreckage. See, the thing is, if we live our whole lives trying desperately to be ships then we miss out on the beauty of our true design as a piece of art.

I wish I had the eloquence with which to express that which aches in my heart to be said, but then again, that might just defeat the whole point. I beg of you do not forsake the brokenness. Refocus and retrain your mind to see the beauty in broken. Walk amongst the wreckage with the Artist and watch as all things are made new.

I am restless with anticipation that the stories between these pages might encourage you to see both your broken beginning and your present whole identity. I am desperate for you to know the greatness of Grace that will simultaneously ruin your best efforts at perfection and restore your greatest failures. I have come to know that it is both demolition of me and construction of me. That may be the most beautiful thing about it-- that it is both wreckage and restoration and I am left with no other choice but to be overcome by it. I urge you to let yourself be overcome by it too.

Special Thanks

Joe & Cheryl Langley: Thank you for not only acknowledging grace with your lips but also expressing it in your lifestyle. I could write pages and pages on how much your friendship has meant to me and they would still not contain it.

Betty Freeman: Thank you for teaching me the true limitlessness of God and His intimate ability to speak the language of the individual. You deepen my understanding of both God's grace and His sovereignty.

Lane Farr: Thank you for standing the gap for me and for truly being a mighty man of God.

Dr. Travis: Thank you for so many things, but hugely for teaching me to befriend my emotions and not to fear them. Thank you for both accepting me as I am and helping me grow. You have taught me shades of grace that I didn't even know were on the color wheel.

Kari McHam & Jesus Dave: Thank you for being badass Jesus freaks who teach me every day how to be fiercely real and love relentlessly.

CHECK OUT JESS'S
FIRST BOOK

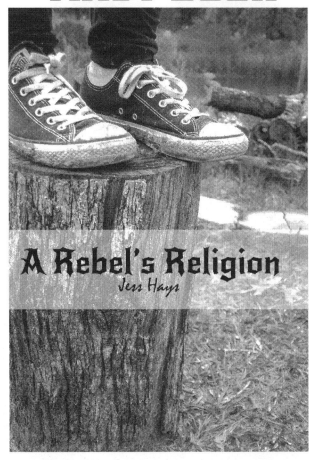

ON AMAZON!

Made in the USA
Charleston, SC
19 July 2016